Praise for *Humanity Works Better*

"*Humanity Works Better* is a practical guide for making people productive in today's disruptive world. Debbie Cohen and Kate Roeske-Zummer have leveraged their extensive experience to develop a step-by-step approach for building trust and holding people accountable. This book presents simple techniques for changing your culture, starting with you."

HOMA BAHRAMI, professor, Haas School of Business, University of California, Berkeley

"*Humanity Works Better* offers concrete evidence for how investing in your people's well-being today will have a direct impact on your bottom line. Equipping us with the courage to let go of what is no longer working for us, this book gives us the refreshing opportunity to explore our vulnerability as a strength in the path to productivity. Required reading for every leader."

KATHERINE HOUSTON, president and CEO, Synopsys Outreach Foundation

"Truly thought-provoking. The real-world examples that demonstrate how to create meaningful change make reading this book the highest and best use of your time. We use the Five Practices every day, and they work!"

MIKE ROBIRDS, co-founder and CEO, Charge EPC

"*Humanity Works Better* changed my understanding of my job as a CEO and plants a bold stake in the ground for leading with humanity. Every CEO should read this book and prepare to have their eyes opened to a new, compassionate way of working."

TYLER BOSMENY, CEO, Clever Inc.

"*Humanity Works Better* is a manifestation of passion becoming purpose. Debbie Cohen and Kate Roeske-Zummer have been championing this kind of work for decades. Their book reinforces that change starts with YOU. Their Five Practices offer straightforward, no-nonsense skills to begin your personal transformation."

HENRY KIMSEY-HOUSE, co-founder, Co-Active
Training Institute; co-author, *Co-Active Coaching*

"Leadership is essentially a human endeavor and rarely does significance happen within and outside organizations without renewed human energy. *Humanity Works Better* gives you the resources to multiply energy, in yourself and others, on purpose. Savor this book!"

KEVIN CASHMAN, global co-leader,
CEO and executive development, Korn Ferry;
author, *Leadership from the Inside Out*

"A decade ago Debbie Cohen and Kate Roeske-Zummer created a huge impact with the work they did at Mozilla. My life has been changed by the concepts in this book. I encourage you to put these 'relationship first' practices into action to amplify yourself and your organization."

JIM COOK, founder and managing director, BenchBoard

"Productivity is about people. *Humanity Works Better*'s Five Practices make complex ideas approachable with actionable steps to help each of us become better humans at work and in life. This book is a must-read."

AARON HURST, founder, Taproot Foundation
and Imperative; author, *The Purpose Economy*

HUMANITY
WORKS
BETTER

5 Practices to Lead with

Awareness, Choice and

the Courage to Change

DEBBIE COHEN &
KATE ROESKE-ZUMMER

HUMANITY WORKS BETTER

PAGE TWO

Cataloguing in publication information is
available from Library and Archives Canada.
ISBN 978-1-77458-050-9 (paperback)
ISBN 978-1-77458-051-6 (ebook)

Page Two
pagetwo.com

Edited by Kendra Ward
Copyedited by Tilman Lewis
Proofread by Alison Strobel
Cover, interior design, and illustrations by Fiona Lee
Printed and bound in Canada by Friesens
Distributed in Canada by Raincoast Books
Distributed in the US and internationally by Macmillan

21 22 23 24 25   5 4 3 2 1

humanityworks.com

Debbie: *To my family and dearest friends*

who have championed me to be

more than I ever thought I could be.

Kate: *For my two biggest champions,*

my dad and George.

CONTENTS

introduction

IMAGINE WHAT IT feels like to work in a place that treats people like human beings, not resources. Imagine what is possible when *how* you work together is just as important as *what* work you do. Imagine working in an organization where people and profits are equally valued. This is a place where humanity works—and this is what we want for you and the people you work with.

Humanity Works Better was written to help you and your organizations improve workplace productivity. Working together is messy and most people don't know how to navigate it well. This results in behaviors that create toxicity and roadblocks that stall productivity. Yet when working together is deeper and more connected, people give more of themselves and business wins.

You can tell if humanity is at work by looking at the quality and depth of workplace relationships. We realized the significance of this in 2005 while working with a large Silicon Valley tech company.

We were working with a team of thirty directors and their boss. The team wanted to work more effectively as a group. At the end of our first day together, we led an evening exercise on vulnerability, modified from Patrick Lencioni's great work

Getting Naked. Each person was asked to come prepared to talk about a personal quality that was both a positive and a negative, and to share something that was going on in their lives that the rest of the group might not know about. The exercise asked participants to be vulnerable, which typically isn't common or easy in a workplace environment.

There were these two guys. Both brilliant engineers, close in age and from similar cultural backgrounds. It was evident from their interactions that they were each other's nemeses as well as each other's biggest fans. These two men had spent long nights together trying to solve some of the biggest technology challenges facing the organization, at times even staying overnight and sleeping underneath their desks to deliver on a product deadline.

One of them, we will call him Jonah, started his story by describing his background, his marriage and the birth of his beloved daughter. He and his wife began noticing their daughter, who was four years old, had a cold that just would not go away. As he was talking, the room got quieter and quieter. His colleague, we will call him Nik, leaned in a little closer. Jonah shared how he and his wife had taken their little girl to a multitude of doctors and specialists. The long and the short of it was their little girl had been diagnosed with leukemia. They did not know what the outcome would be. And that is where his story ended for that evening.

As he concluded, you could have heard a pin drop in the room. When someone is sharing their story, we ask others to stay silent, not to ask questions, interrupt or crosstalk. The role of the listeners is to be present with that person, to witness them and the story they are telling. Soon it was time for a break. Nik approached Jonah and hugged him, saying, "I had no idea you were dealing with this. I am so sorry." The two left the room deep in conversation.

In that moment, the purpose of HumanityWorks—our coaching, consulting and training organization—crystalized. We saw it so clearly. Something is terribly wrong with our work relationships if people are literally sleeping on the floor next to their colleagues and have no idea what is happening for them as human beings. Everyone in that room was impacted by genuinely witnessing one another. They began to see their co-workers as more complex human beings. They were more aware that when they share the more vulnerable sides of their life, a deeper human connection is created. That each of them leads a rich, full, complex life of which work is just one part.

We are on a mission to bring more humanity to the workplace and to you as a leader, so we can change the world of work together. This fundamental goal is what drove us to create HumanityWorks, and it's what underpins the research, stories and practices we offer you in this book. At HumanityWorks we focus on the traits that help people demonstrate the qualities of being a good human. We think one of the core ways of being a good human, and a good leader, is by caring about people around you; this creates a connection that not only makes working together more fulfilling but also paves the way to doing great things.

Think about it: the backbone of any good relationship is that you know that a person cares about you. This knowledge is the lens through which you evaluate everything a person says and does, be it positive or negative. If you know in your heart that someone cares about you, then you trust what they say, and that can motivate you to act. If you do not think that they care about you, then you can get triggered and react negatively to any action or word that they utter. This begins a downward spiral in any relationship. It boosts the assumption-making machines within. You start to invent stories about why they said what they said; you begin to pull back or defend yourself;

you find yourself some allies and build your case against your nemesis; you resist working with the other person... You are officially triggered, trust is gone and a productive working relationship is out the window.

At the heart of the HumanityWorks movement, and this book, is you. If things are not quite right in your workplace, the real change starts with you. Being a leader, in its fullest expression, is about continuity of character. That is what makes people want to work with you, to follow you—and it helps you get stuff done. If you want to be a better leader, start with awareness: How are you being with others? How do you choose to show up? How does that affect those around you?

Being a leader is about having the courage to let go of what is not serving you and stepping into a more impactful way of leading. As a leader, you have tremendous influence on the people of your organization. People deserve a workplace where they are valued as humans, not resources. And when humanity works better, the workplace thrives.

Getting Work Done, Better

This book will guide your journey to becoming aware of who you want to be and choosing how to live the whole of your life, inside and outside the workplace, to be consistent with those beliefs. It lays out the case for why more humanity is needed at work today, but it goes beyond the why—it's also a how-to book. It provides skills and tools to help you navigate the complex relationships that make us human beings, complexities that often become the roadblocks that make it hard to get important work done.

In part 1, we look at productivity and mindset. According to 21st Century Skills, which provides students with the

If things are not quite right in your workplace, **the real change starts with you. Being a leader, in its fullest expression, is about continuity of character.**

essential skills, knowledge and expertise needed to be successful throughout their life, productivity is the ability to create a
product by setting and meeting goals, prioritizing needs, managing time, working ethically, collaborating and cooperating
with colleagues and clients.[1] Goals, prioritization and time
management are tried and true methods to achieve productivity outcomes like alignment and accountability. The "softer"
skills of working ethically, in collaboration and with cooperation reflect the growing importance of how we work together to
drive essential productivity outcomes like trust, resiliency and
engagement. A big roadblock to embracing the "softer" skills
can be how you think about things—your mindset. Your mindset is a reflection of your attitudes and beliefs, which influence
your behaviors. It takes attention and awareness to shift mindsets that hold you back from being the person you want to be.

In part 2, we take a deep dive into the five fundamental
practices that teach leaders and the people in their organizations exactly how to build the muscle required to work together
productively as human beings. These practices offer insight
into your behaviors and the practical skills and tools for action:

- **Creating safety** builds trust.
- **Working together** manifests resilience.
- **Claiming values** produces alignment.
- **Owning your impact** drives accountability.
- **Daring not to know** creates engagement.

These Five Practices put people first. They are how you
deepen your connections with the people around you so you
can be more productive. They are the magic for success and
drive unrealized business results. This book will help *you*
produce these outcomes. Good humans doing good work,
increasing productivity and organizational strength: humanity works better.

This book has the potential to change you. It will make you more aware of yourself. It will challenge you to try new skills and ways of thinking about yourself and those around you. It will ignite a desire to change things about yourself, things that are holding you back from being the kind of human you want to be.

Change is courageous and hard work. So be gentle with yourself. You are unlearning, unlocking yourself and building new muscle. You will have good days and bad days. You will have exciting moments when you are conscious of your competence: you are doing it and it is working. And you will have harder days, when it does not work. Be patient. Change takes time and practice, practice, practice.

PART 1

WHERE BETTER WORK BEGINS

1

productivity— it's all about people

A GREAT DEAL OF business focus in the 1990s and early 2000s was on efficiency: cut the fat, work lean. This created solid business results. As Michael Mankins writes in his article "Great Companies Obsess Over Productivity, Not Efficiency": "Earnings growth for the S&P 500 ran at nearly three times the rate of inflation over this period, despite tepid top-line growth in many years." In effect, companies reduced the cost of doing business and found financial gains. Around 2015 this strategy stopped working. Mankins continues: "Without top-line growth, continuing to wring out greater profits through efficiency has become the managerial equivalent of attempting to squeeze blood from a stone."[1]

So, business pivoted from a focus on efficiency to a focus on productivity. If efficiency is about "less is more," productivity is about "doing more with the same." Productivity is the rate of output per unit of input. The concept hearkens back to a time when people worked on factory lines and their value was measured by the time it took to produce a single item. Envision being a factory line worker where the speed of the conveyor belt is turned up and you are expected to turn up your output accordingly. Those who could not keep up were replaced. While humans may not have benefited, this approach served business well during the manufacturing and mass production era.

In today's knowledge-based economy, productivity faces at least two challenges the earlier era did not: a shortage of talent and a burgeoning awareness that the intellectual capital of talent walks out the door when they leave at the end of each day—or when they quit for good. In March 2019, pre-pandemic, Vox reported a widespread worker shortage in the United States. In the decades leading up to 2020, there had been more available workers than available jobs. However, by the end of January 2020, things were beginning to shift. The US economy had 7.6 million unfilled jobs, but only 6.5 million people were looking for work, according to data released by the US Bureau of Labor Statistics.[2] This was the eleventh straight month that the number of job openings was higher than the number of job seekers. Each month the gap grew. Recovery from the historic unemployment rates experienced during the pandemic will slow the effect of the labor shortage for a while, but the reality of the shortage remains and is looming. There are too few people for too many jobs. With baby boomers retiring en masse and a replacement workforce in short supply, it is no longer a viable approach to productivity to simply demand that fewer people produce more.

Since the push for heightened productivity began in 2015, the unrelenting demands to get more out of people are taking mental and physical tolls on the humans doing the work, at tremendous costs to both employees and companies. Humans are reaching their breaking point. The effect is a burned out, demotivated, detached, overworked workforce. You've seen them. You might even be part of this group.

In this type of workforce, it's hard to get work done because people go in and out of the organization through a revolving door. People just don't care, and they deflect responsibility, which makes it really tough to get good work done. The politics of fear and competition becomes toxic and cutthroat, making it feel unsafe for people to raise up their heads, much less share an idea or take a risk.

Micromanagement happens because failure to deliver is not an option. Members of this group do not feel seen, heard or recognized; they just do what is needed until they see a clear path to somewhere else. The human spirit detaches. Folks might show up, but their minds and hearts and souls are somewhere else. When self-interests overtake principles, uncivil behavior seeps into the lifeblood of an organization and civility is lost.

Civility is a mindset you hold about other human beings. Marilyn Price-Mitchell notes in *Psychology Today* that civility is a personal attitude that acknowledges other humans' rights to live and co-exist in a manner that does not harm others.[3] Civility calls for tolerance of differences and respect for one another.

This concept of civility might sound lovely on paper, but we have all worked in too many places where the "no-asshole rule" was simply given lip service. Debbie recounts a time when she was part of a post-merger integration team. She and a colleague from "the other company" were tapped to conduct diversity and inclusion (D&I) training for the newly formed top of the house: C-suite and senior executives. As the day proceeded, the participants were nice, even polite. They dutifully went along with what was asked of them. From Debbie's perspective, they were biding their time until the clock ran out.

As they neared the end of the session, she couldn't resist; she had to put the elephant on the table. "I'm curious. If our top salesperson exhibits toxic behaviors in violation of these standards, what actions will happen?" Without blinking, a top executive in the room looked right at her and stated, "Nothing." Unfortunately, this is not an isolated story. When folks simply go through the motions, checking the box of compliance and giving lip service to its meaning, the outcome is harmful. And for too many, the outcome of tolerated toxic behavior in the workplace is all too familiar.

Christine Porath is a professor of management and the author of *Mastering Civility: A Manifesto for the Workplace*. Her research in nearly every industry and type of organization has disclosed rampant, widespread incivility. In the past twenty years, she has polled thousands of people: 98 percent report experiencing uncivil behavior and 99 percent have witnessed it. More than half of respondents do not report issues of incivility out of fear or a sense of helplessness. "We all want to come to work and be treated with kindness and respect," she notes.[4]

When insecurities have no constructive way to evolve, they erupt into threats, intimidation and bullying. In April 2017, the Workplace Bullying Institute studied the prevalence of abusive behaviors in the workplace. Their findings indicate abusive behaviors in the workplace are at an "epidemic level":

- 30 million American workers have been, or are now being, bullied at work; one in five US workers is a victim.

- Another 30 million American workers (again, one in five) have witnessed bullying behaviors in the workplace.

- 63 percent of respondents are aware that workplace bullying happens.[5]

In his article "Diagnose and Eliminate Workplace Bullying," Baron Christopher Hanson claims, "Whether it's an entrenched dinosaur or extreme ladder-climber, anyone who manipulates selfish outcomes or seeks unfair advantage must be confronted expediently. Bullies are tremendously expensive for corporations in terms of productivity and talents lost. When C-suites overlook blatant bullying, work is sabotaged, progress is blocked, and company value may be lost or stolen."[6]

The impact of all of this on productivity? According to Gallup's *State of the Global Workplace* study, "85% of employees worldwide are not engaged or actively disengaged in their job." Disengaged employees are harmful to the workplace.

They complain constantly but aren't interested in resolving problems or improving things. They are frustrated and openly share their feelings through destructive passive-aggressive behaviors, gossip and lying. On teams, they dodge attempts at outreach and are unwilling to help others.

Disengaged employees tend to separate themselves from others, going rogue and acting on their own. Tension swirls around them and erupts, with their manager, their team, their leadership. Gallup estimates actively disengaged employees cost US companies between $450 billion and $550 billion in lost productivity per year.[7]

A Workplace Where People Thrive

Working with others is messy. Most people don't know how to navigate it well. This results in wrong behaviors that create roadblocks and toxicity that can stall productivity. As a leader of your team and in your organization, it's important to pause and reflect on how you, yourself, may create roadblocks or enable toxic behavior. Your people are watching you all the time, taking cues from what you do and say. They look to you to make work deeper and more connected, and when it is, people give more of themselves and business wins. The 2015 Gallup report *State of the American Manager* notes that managers account for at least a 70 percent variance in employee engagement.[8] The question we ask at HumanityWorks is how to amplify your impact, how to deepen the connection between you and the humans in your organizations, so together you can achieve more.

Emma Seppälä and Kim Cameron highlight the importance of this movement in their article "Proof That Positive Work Cultures Are More Productive."[9] Their work advocates for employee well-being and its impact on productivity. They

Reflect on where or how

you may create roadblocks or enable toxic behavior.

assert that well-being comes from only one place—a positive workplace culture. Their research identified six essential characteristics of a positive and healthy workplace culture:

- Caring for, being interested in and maintaining responsibility for colleagues as friends.

- Providing support for one another, including offering kindness and compassion when others are struggling.

- Avoiding blame and forgiving mistakes.

- Inspiring one another at work.

- Emphasizing the meaningfulness of the work.

- Treating one another with respect, gratitude, trust and integrity.[10]

Seppälä and Cameron note: "When organizations develop positive, virtuous cultures they achieve significantly higher levels of organizational effectiveness—including financial performance, customer satisfaction, productivity, and employee engagement."[11] Adam Grant, in his book *Give and Take*, further highlights productivity gains found from cultivating a positive workplace culture. He showcases the connection between team and organizational outcomes and the need from leaders to demonstrate positive human characteristics such as kindness and generosity.[12] In today's dramatically reconfigured world of work, success is increasingly dependent on how we interact with others.

In the fall of 2019, we participated in a fascinating "disruptor" dinner party. A disruptor dinner is when you invite folks with different backgrounds and perspectives to discuss a particular topic that you want to think about in a different way—in other words, to disrupt! At this disruptor dinner the focus was human potential. Folks talked about the time continuum and new ideas that would help organizations with just-in-time learning, as well as ideas for robotics and artificial intelligence. It was fascinating.

The guy whose product was about just-in-time learning, a platform designed to improve communication and build human connection, gave an example of what that might look like. He illustrated one use of the tool—it could inform a manager based in one country about an upcoming statutory holiday in a different country where the manager had an employee. Without the prompt, the manager would not know that the employee should have time off and would proceed with business as usual. With this prompt, the manager could proactively inquire about the employee's plans and coordinate time away accordingly. We loved that idea. What a simple way to help two people connect.

Someone in the group challenged him, asking, "Great, that would definitely help their relationship, but how does it help improve productivity?" The guy whose product this was paused before answering the question. Kate had been listening quietly up until that moment. Then it was like someone lit a fire under her. She erupted, "Because people are more likely to work harder if they feel like their boss gives a shit about them! Productivity requires people working at their best. If you have a better relationship with the people around you, you are more likely to work harder if asked. We all think that people should just work harder, but the truth is, sometimes they will and sometimes they won't."

CHG Healthcare is one example of a large organization that created an environment for employees to thrive by putting people first. During the recession from 2008 to 2011, while the profitability of its industry peers declined, CHG Healthcare grew revenue and profits. With turnover less than half the industry average, it is the most profitable company in the healthcare staffing industry—and it is known as a great place to work.[13]

From our experience with organizations of all sizes around the globe, we know there is unrealized potential inside your organization, and likely in your team. To fully realize that potential, a shift needs to occur. Attention needs to turn away from using processes and procedures as the levers to productivity and focus first on the people who make those outputs possible. Companies need people who are resilient and can work constructively to navigate and thrive through any change an organization experiences.

What Is at Risk?

You cannot open the news without reading about a leader's impending dismissal for not being a good human: Intel and Priceline CEOs were let go because of inappropriate relationships with women employees, American Apparel's CEO was let go for sexual harassment, Best Buy's CEO Brian Dunn was let go for indiscretions with a female employee.[14] In mid-2020, Greg Glassman of CrossFit was let go because of his conspiracy theories and denial of systemic racial discrimination. Then there's the story of the CEO of Away, the luggage and travel company, who, it was reported, "was infamous for tearing into people on Slack," leaving people in tears.[15] We dive into this dramatic example of toxic workplace culture further in chapter 3. When poor behavior starts at the top, the effects are felt all the way through the organization.

Unfortunately, this may be an all-too-common situation, where those at the top are too distanced from the humans who are doing the work of the company. And the effect is not just emotional or interpersonal. IBM, in combination with WorkHuman, published a white paper called *The Financial Impact of a Positive Employee Experience*. After compiling previous surveys and interviews from nearly 24,000 people in forty-five countries, they found:

- Organizations that score in the top 25 percent on employee experience report nearly three times the return on assets compared to organizations in the bottom quartile.

- Organizations that score in the top 25 percent on employee experience report double the return on sales compared to organizations in the bottom quartile.[16]

It is time to look for a different way to drive productivity. Productivity is about people. Enough with efficiency and process reinvention. There is nothing more to squeeze out of folks, and the data proves it. Folks are burned out, disengaged, unwell and just don't care. It doesn't have to be that way. As a leader of your team, and in your organization, you and your team contribute to the workplace culture. If things are not quite right, you are part of the solution. Which is why *you* are at the center of our movement where humanity works better.

Change starts with you because the only thing you can actually control in life is yourself. You can become more aware of what you do and how you are with others. With this insight, as a leader, when you shift how you interact with others, you will ignite change in them.

In part 2, our Five Practices provide straightforward techniques to develop insight into your behaviors, and practical skills and tools for action. Our Five Practices are:

- **Creating safety:** The most important aspect of working with people is to create an environment that feels safe, physically and psychologically. And it's up to you.

- **Working together:** A big perspective shift is to let go of your personal agenda and focus on the common goal. The secret to working together is it's not about you.

- **Claiming values:** Claiming values means knowing what you stand for, your nonnegotiables. Know what is important to you.

- **Owning your impact:** This is how people experience you, what makes you compelling and what people say about you when you are not in the room. Be responsible for what you create.

- **Daring not to know:** This is the practice of surrender—it paves the way for deeper engagement and loyalty from others. You lead the way.

These practices increase your self-awareness, and from this place you can stand in choice about how you are behaving with the people you work with. You show the way. When you have the courage to change, you help your organization be more human, and by doing so, you make humanity work better.

Before we look at the Five Practices in depth, however, we need to look at an essential quality for fueling human potential and possibility: a growth mindset.

2

shifting your mindset to embrace change

W E WISH CHANGE were easy... learn a few new skills and be a better human. Unfortunately, it's not that simple. But it does not have to be hard, either, if you are open and willing. Most organizational advice tells you what to do: "establish trust," "be transparent," "be authentic." You've read those books and been to those trainings. Organizations are filled with one-and-done, flavor-of-the-month trainings intended to make you do something differently.

Telling you what to do rarely works to create behavior change. You can learn to mimic behavior, but mimicking the behavior of others does not help you become conscious of why you are doing what you are doing. And doing isn't enough. It requires a conscious effort to be a good human, an effort to align who you are being with what you are doing. Changing behavior requires a shift in your mindset, how you think about things, coupled with a willingness and a desire to be different, to consciously act in accordance with the person you want to be.

Your mindset is an established set of attitudes, a habitual, embedded way of thinking. Let's play with this a bit. Consider the topic of intelligence. What are your thoughts about it? In your way of thinking, is intelligence a factor of your genetics, something you are born with? Or is intelligence formed from hard work and effort, something you can grow? Are talents and abilities limited or do people have the capacity to grow and change?

In her book *Mindset*, Carol Dweck asks, "What are the consequences of thinking your intelligence or personality is something you can develop, as opposed to something that is a fixed, deep-seated trait?"[1] When you hold a mindset, for yourself or for others, that particular characteristics, attributes or qualities are predetermined, you will behave in a limited or "fixed" way of being. Dweck claims, "In a fixed mindset, people believe their basic qualities, like their intelligence or talent, are simply fixed traits. They spend their time documenting their intelligence or talent instead of developing them. They also believe that talent alone creates success—without effort. They're wrong."[2] Dweck's research identified a second type of mindset, one that is generative. She calls this a "growth mindset" and defines it as follows: "In a growth mindset, people believe that their most basic abilities can be developed through dedication and hard work—brains and talent are just the starting point. This view creates a love of learning and a resilience that is essential for great accomplishments. Virtually all great people have had these qualities."[3]

Consider how Dweck's research shows up in you and in your workplace. Do attitudes and behaviors represent more of a fixed mindset that fuels limiting traits like blame, shame, unhealthy competition, passivity, politics and toxic behaviors? Or do they exhibit a growth mindset where possibility, iterative learning, resilience, generosity and deep connection are supported? To be a good human and do good work, we assert that a growth mindset is essential as it fuels human potential and possibility. So, now what (particularly if you have a fixed mindset)?

Mindsets are learned. They are influenced by your experiences and the societal messages you receive. They are shaped by the culture and the environment you grew up in. They have molded your current identity, how you perceive yourself and the world around you. Your mindset shapes your attitudes and beliefs and drives your behavior. It is the dominant factor in how you act in the world.

You, like most humans, are probably unconscious of the fact that your mindset is the driver of your life, steering your words and behaviors. When you step back and consider the implications, it's truly amazing that you can be so unaware of something with such a powerful influence. In most cases, you have not consciously chosen your mindset; it is embedded within you. So, if there is something about yourself, like how you are being in the world, that doesn't seem quite right with you, changing it starts with you. In the words of Master Yoda from *Star Wars*, "You must unlearn what you have learned!" When it comes to being human and doing good work, becoming aware of and standing in choice of your attitudes, beliefs and actions is essential to your personal development and performance.[4] You are in control—that's the good news.

The not-so-good news is that mindsets are resistant to change. Robert Kegan and Lisa Laskow Lahey have spent the last twenty-five-plus years researching, studying, teaching and writing on the topic of adult learning and professional development. They have discovered that behind most habits are indelible attitudes and beliefs that not only keep you from moving forward but also protect you from any kind of change that might threaten the status quo. Your identity is shaped by your beliefs, and it works hard to protect itself—even when it is holding you back from who you want to become. This resistance is so strong that Kegan and Lahey have likened it to an "immune system" whose job is to recognize and eliminate threats.[5] Based on unspoken assumptions you have about yourself and the world, you can unknowingly resist change, because change feels unsafe.

It takes attention and awareness to shift attitudes and beliefs that hold you back from being the person you want to be. To get started, you need to wake up to what you are thinking and why. To effectively step into a new behavior, you need to look at the beliefs that drive that behavior.

The rest of this chapter introduces four possible shifts from fixed mindsets to growth mindsets:

- From problem-reacting to **outcome-creating.**
- From erecting barriers to keep people out to **creating boundaries to let people in.**
- From struggling with resistance to **navigating resistance.**
- From self-interest to **meaningful connections.**

In part 2 we will provide opportunities to explore the four growth mindsets within our Five Practices. Self-reflection exercises, practical tools and techniques will give you insights for how to move ideas into action that will help you be a good human and do better work.

Outcome-Creating

There are two life stances: problem-reacting, used to keep you safe and playing small, and outcome-creating, used to bring something you care about into being. Problem-reacting focuses on removing what you do not want (issues, obstacles, threats), so that you just stop what is undesirable, make it go away. Outcome-creating focuses on generating what you want. It is where systemic, long-term solutions are developed. This mindset shifts your intentions. You focus on bringing something new into being. If you are usually super-busy doing work or reacting to someone else's agenda but never feel like you are moving things forward, then outcome-creating may be a mindset for you to explore in greater depth. Both problem-reacting and outcome-creating can serve you, but they do so in very different ways.

It takes attention and awareness to shift attitudes and beliefs that hold you back from being the person you want to be.

Before we explore outcome-creating in depth, let's spend some time with problem-reacting. You may be familiar with the concept of the fight-flight-freeze response. This response gets triggered as your body's natural reaction to situations that feel unsafe, dangerous or threatening. The stress response that takes place within your body causes hormonal and physiological changes. The internal tension and discomfort that you feel is hard-wired into your body; it is an unconscious response.

The Leadership Circle Profile is an amazing organization that has compiled a vast treasure trove of tools and resources for their coaching community. They have incorporated the work of forward thinkers Robert Fritz and Karen Horney, who evolved the concepts of flight-flight-freeze into "reactive tendencies."[6] When you are in a reactive tendency, you are focused on one thing: stopping what you do not want. It might be a problem, an obstacle or a threat. When your reactive tendency drives your behavior, you move away from the problem that is bothering you or, more precisely, from the unpleasant emotions generated by the problem, to make it go away. When you are in a reactive stance, your goal is to get "back to normal," back to where you started from as quickly as possible.

There are three primary reactive tendencies: complying, protecting and controlling. Often people gravitate to one or two of these reactive types. Remember, your reactive tendency is triggered when you feel threatened:

- **Compliers** want to avoid conflict and disharmony. This is the "freeze" mentality. You get a sense of security by complying with the expectations of others rather than acting on what you want. You tend to relinquish power to others and to the circumstances in your life to keep harmony and peace. You see the world as full of powerful people who can control or protect you, and your self-worth is linked to their approval. With this mindset, you tend to go along with those in authority, obeying their requests and following their expectations. You do this to gain safety and win approval.

- **Protectors** want to avoid closeness. This is the "flight" mentality. You get a sense of worth through feeling superior and/or rational. You keep yourself safe by staying aloof and maintaining distance in your relationships. This stance can come from an inner self-doubt, inferiority or lack of confidence, or its opposite, self-assurance or superiority. You might project an air of arrogance, need to be right, find fault and put others down in an effort to build yourself up. Your internal set of assumptions link security with distance, and worth with either being small and uninvolved or big and superior.

- **Controllers** want to avoid failure. This is the "fight" mentality. You establish a sense of personal worth through task accomplishment and personal achievement. You strive to take charge, be on top and exert control over others in order to gain self-worth, personal safety and identity. You see the world as made up of winners and losers, where powerful people stand the best chance, so, to survive, you must be one of the winners. Completing tasks is the key to your sense of accomplishment. You must excel heroically, be perfect, perform flawlessly and/or dominate.[7]

So, what is the issue with a problem-reacting mindset? No problem, if back to normal is where you want to go. There are times when problem-reacting serves you and those around you. Consider times of real disasters, when you are under threat, like when a building is on fire. Controllers will step in and help get folks out safely. Compliers will know what the evacuation protocol is and follow along so that the building can be quickly vacated. Protectors will hold the bigger picture for what needs to happen in the crisis and lead the group through it. Working together under duress and times of crisis, these reactive tendencies can serve you and those around you well.

More often, though, you are not in life-threating crisis. But you are in a dynamic, rapidly evolving world and workplace where situations around you constantly change. It can feel unsettling. You are stretching—new situations, new learnings, new growth. In these times your "immune system" kicks in. Your reactive tendency tries to protect you from the change that growth creates, to quiet the discomfort, the threat and the disorientation that is part of evolving as humans. Your internal regulator tries to shuttle you back to normal.

Back to normal is in the past. Circumstances within and/or around you have started to evolve. Your role in the workplace is generally not to maintain normalcy, it is to create a new future reality—to move things forward. This is hard, uncomfortable work. You do not grow from a place of comfort; discomfort is the catalyst for change. What you can do is become aware of and familiar with your reactive tendencies so that when they appear you can assess the circumstance for what it is. And from there, be in conscious choice about how or if back to normal serves you. You choose.

Awareness starts with understanding which reactive tendency is your default mode. Pause for a minute and reread the three reactive tendencies above: compliers, protectors, controllers. Which one feels most familiar to you? Consider different situations. Recall a physical or emotional crisis you have experienced—how did you react? What about at work when stuff hits the fan, tempers are flying and all around you seems chaotic—how do you react? There is no right or wrong answer. There is no better or worse tendency. What's important is to know your default and become aware of it. The Leadership

Circle Profile 360 tool is a more comprehensive way to identify your reactive tendencies and gain insight on how they may be limiting your potential.[8]

Outcome-creating is a growth mindset that enables you to step into a situation and actively create the outcome you want. In outcome-creating, you act out of desire to generate something new. Creating inevitably brings up doubt, stress or anxiety. Unanticipated problems will pop up. When you are in outcome-creating mode, you take on these issues, looking for the possibility in the challenge rather than viewing it as a problem. You remain undaunted in your quest to create an envisioned outcome. Momentum and meaning are created by focusing your attention on the actions that achieve your desired results.

Better Outcome-Creating

When you are ready to look for new possibilities to the challenge you are facing, ask yourself:

- What is my vision for the best possible outcome for this situation?
- What excites me about this vision?
- How does having this vision change how I am going to approach this situation?

_____

_____

_____

_____

You are training the people around you all the time

how to treat you.

Instead of being driven by conflict or problems you don't want, you are motivated by meaning and passion and what matters to you. You are excited about the potential outcome you are striving for, and that energy propels you forward. You are not motivated to make something go away so that you can get back to normal, but rather, you are motivated to bring something new into existence. You have stepped into an internal narrative, a mindset of possibility and of being powerful.

Creating Boundaries

Boundaries are one of the most neglected and misunderstood concepts in the workplace. Too often thought of (and practiced) as policies outlining "the rules" that must be followed, barriers are created that reek of mistrust, assuming the worst in humanity. Here's the shift: boundaries are there to let people in—not keep people out. They are generated from a sense of shared well-being and set forth what is needed to create safe, permissible interactions. And they state the natural and logical consequences should boundaries fail to be honored. They create a workplace where everyone feels safe to fully contribute and participate.

Boundaries are one of the first things we talk about when we work with leaders of organizations. Boundaries, at their best, establish clear guidelines around behavior that create a sense of safety and well-being and are essential for forming authentic trust.

You have to know your own boundaries: What are you okay with, and why? What are you not okay with, and what's important about that? For you and for those trying to work with you, the cost of not being clear about your boundaries is stress, burnout, exhaustion and resentment. If these are symptoms in your life, it might be beneficial to examine your mindset with boundaries. The truth is, they have to begin with you.

We have a phrase that you will hear more than once from us: "You are training the people around you all the time how to treat you." Years ago, during Kate's time as an account executive in a big New York City advertising agency, she was working on a new business pitch for a fast-food chain. There was a senior ad exec who had a bit of a reputation as a "Good Old Boy." He would often hold court in the company cafeteria with a bunch of other young men. (At that time, it really was all men!)

Kate and a colleague of hers, Ralph, had partnered with a local nonprofit so that folks within the agency could sign up to volunteer, using their lunch hour to deliver a hot meal to people in the neighborhood with AIDS. She and Ralph were actively recruiting volunteers and had created a poster that was displayed in front of the cafeteria. On this particular day, the senior ad exec, we will call him Joe, waved Kate over to his table, where he was sitting at the head with eight to ten guys around him. He proceeded to tell Kate off, berating her and the meal delivery program, and yelling at her to take the poster down before the fast-food chain clients came to town, which was going to be in about a week. Kate will never repeat what he actually said because it was so inexplicably rude. Holding her tray of food, she started to shake, then she turned around and left. She was in shock. She bumped into Ralph and explained what had just happened. He said, "You have to talk to HR." So, Kate left to find the head of HR.

Now, here's the deal. She did not know what she wanted to do. In the moments and hours after this experience, she did not know "the answer." She just knew one thing: she did not want the senior exec to think he could talk to her, or for that matter anyone else in the agency, like that again. That's it.

That's all she knew. The head of HR was terrific. She said that his behavior was illegal and that they could file a complaint, but she left the choice up to Kate. "What do you want?" she asked Kate. And for the first time, Kate was able to say out loud, "I don't want him thinking he can talk to me or anyone else like that." The head of HR said, "Then you have to go and tell him that."

So she did. Kate went to his office. He was alone. No posse to grandstand with. She asked if they could talk. He meekly replied, "Yes." Kate told him that the way that he talked to her in the cafeteria was illegal. And that he could never talk to her or anyone else like that again. If he did, she would file charges against him. He said, "Okay." She left his office. He never did talk like that to her again. In fact, she never worked with him again. Probably his choice as much as her own.

Kate was a junior ad exec at this time. Does she think that this experience changed the senior exec? No, not really. However, after talking to HR, Kate felt supported and safe enough to confront him. And her actions may have made a difference for others. You can take a stand for what you (and others) need to feel safe. This experience became a guiding beacon for Kate, a standard for how to draw boundaries. It became one way for her to apply her own internal listening. What was important to her? What was she okay with? What was she not okay with? This clarity allowed her to live her life and behave from a place of personal integrity, to stay in relationship with herself.

Better Boundaries

To learn more about your boundaries and what is most important to you, ask yourself:

- How do I want to be treated?
- Why is that important to me?
- What is a nonnegotiable for me?
- What is important about that and why?
- What is a choice and what is not a choice?

_____

_____

_____

_____

_____

If you see boundaries as fences to keep others out, as a way to protect you from harm, get curious about what it is that you are trying to protect. What is inside those boundaries that you honor and hold dear? What would it be like to think about boundaries as a way of letting more in, rather than keeping things at bay? Fitness blogger Lana Osborne-Paradis writes: "Setting boundaries does not mean building walls to keep others out, healthy boundaries show people where to find the door. A boundary teaches people how to interact with us in a way that allows us to thrive, feel safe and respected. A wall keeps people out and gives them limited access to creating a relationship with us."[9]

Navigating Resistance

Resistance is a powerful mindset that has many forms: inner resistance, resistance to another, to an idea or to a way forward. Here's what you might not know about resistance: it is most often rooted in fear. Resistance can feel personal and uncomfortable and make you want to distance yourself from it. The mindset shift here is to step towards the resistance and seek to understand what it is about. The knowledge and compassion that result will generate resilience and enable you to navigate through resistance in the future.

One form of inner resistance you may be unconscious of is your personal "saboteurs." They create fear in you and keep you small. Your internal saboteurs are a powerful form of resistance that incite powerful narratives. These stories can dominate you and dictate your action or inaction. Identifying your saboteurs is the first step in familiarizing yourself with them, of inching towards them. The three classic types of saboteurs are directly related to your reactive tendencies:

- **The fear of not being good enough** (hello, compliers). This type of inner resistance shows up when you want to be creative, original and competent, but you notice that little voice taunting you, telling you that you're not good enough and you care a bit too much what others think.

- **The fear of not knowing** (hello, protectors). This inner resistance shows up when you want to be in control, to know the unknowable, to rationalize the inexplicable. This voice scoffs at you, making you question yourself, and ignites feelings of inadequacy.

- **The fear of failure** (hello, controllers). This inner resistance shows up as relentless activity, constant momentum, a need to keep doing. The voice of failure haunts you, whispering that if you just work harder and put in more hours, you won't let others down or experience disappointment.

Your saboteurs will always be a part of you. You just don't want them in the driver's seat of your life. Once you meet your saboteurs, you can take control; you know when they help and when they hold you back from who you want to be in this world. You learn to step towards the fear they create, and you seek meaning there. We coach our clients to become so familiar with their inner resistance that they give their saboteurs names.

Ben Limmer, formerly the solutions architect at Ibotta (and currently a freelance software architect and engineer), knows all about saboteurs and how they can prevent positive leadership attributes from showing up. In his coaching work with Kate, they examined his tendency to worry about the small stuff. Ben became aware that his dominant reactive tendency is to control, that stress is its trigger and that it manifested in perfectionism. He named his saboteur "Mr. Perfect Pants," and in coaching sessions, Kate reinforced Ben's awareness of who was in control by asking questions like, "Is this Mr. Perfect Pants talking, or is it you talking?" During high-stress situations, Ben will practice daily journaling to "slow the F down!" and take things day-to-day, to be more in the moment. This pause helps Ben slow down and provide space for others on his team to step up. Before coaching, Ben never saw himself as a perfectionist and was unaware of how perfectionism influenced his leadership. Now he is conscious of how his saboteur shows up and can limit his leadership capabilities. During periods of high stress, he is more self-aware, is a better leader and can spend time focused on the important things.[10]

Better Navigation of Inner Resistance

Get to know your inner saboteur:

- How does your saboteur show up?
- What is your saboteur afraid of?
- What message is your saboteur telling you?
- Give your saboteur an image.
- Name your saboteur.

_____

_____

_____

_____

_____

This work is about getting the saboteur out of the driver's seat and placing you, the you that knows what you want, into it. Your saboteurs are there to supposedly keep you "safe," when in fact they just keep you small; they repeat old narratives that may have served you once but have outlived their welcome. You do not need them anymore.

Meaningful Connections

The doing of work tends to be self-focused: your goals, your aspirations, your achievements, your success. Meaningful connections shift you from focusing on your own self-interest to thinking about the needs of the collective whole. In the workplace, no one is successful in isolation. Your achievements are closely linked to and interdependent with those of others. When working together is deeper and more connected, people give more of themselves. You and the business win. Decades of research show meaningful connections with the people you work with do more to deepen employee engagement than anything else. This shift helps you, as a team leader or manager, influence the systemic whole.

The Leadership Circle Profile adeptly defines meaningful connection: "You genuinely care about others. People feel supported in your presence because you are open to high quality, trusting, caring relationships. You tend to accept others for who they are and communicate unconditional positive regard. You are willing to vulnerably share strengths and weakness, hopes and fears. Others tend to trust you with these same very human aspects of their selves."[11]

Articulate prides themselves in being a human-centered organization, where one of their key beliefs is: We are all connected, healing and improving ourselves, and our relationships with one another reverberate throughout our teams, society and the world.

The VP of people, Angela Kiniry, notes: "Meaningful connections are at the core of what we are working on at Articulate. When people feel safe, they become more open, more vulnerable." This connection builds trust and is key to working together successfully. Angela continues, "People need to have authentic conversations to move through the messiness that's a given at work, and they need to have these conversations in a way that is safe for everyone."

Articulate has partnered with HumanityWorks to bring a common framework into the organization. A common framework that everyone has committed to is critical to achieving a human-centered organization that can scale. "When things inevitably go off the rails, an agreed-upon framework for working together creates a path for getting back on track."

As the common framework reaches deeper into the organization, Angela has noticed people are becoming more engaged, more vulnerable, wanting to learn and grow, and feeling safe to speak up when things aren't working. "When people feel connected, they are more comfortable voicing their opinions, which are critical inputs in our growing business. Meaningful connections create the bonds of trust that bring out the best in everyone. When people are able to function as their highest and best selves, then Articulate is at its best as well."[12]

Better Connections

Seek to help others know they are seen and understood. Look outside of yourself and ask:

- What is important to them?
- What do they want to create?
- What might be happening for them that you are unaware of?
- How can you best support them?

_____

_____

_____

_____

_____

When your people know they are truly cared for, loved and appreciated, they will work tirelessly to achieve great things. A team's strength and resiliency are bolstered when people feel seen and know that they contribute to a common purpose and their contributions are valued. You are in all sorts of relationships with people at work and in the rest of your life. So it's important to look beyond yourself to how you create meaningful connections with the people around you. When you are in relationships with people that you are not sure of or do not trust, pause and step towards them with curiosity.

Being aware of your mindset and choosing to make a change is big work. It requires a conscious effort to align what you believe with how you are being. Part 2 of *Humanity Works Better* is a deep dive into the Five Practices, our key framework to bring more humanity to your workplace. Within each of the practices, you will see tips to help you align your mindset with practical skills so the best of your leadership can shine.

THE FIVE PRACTICES

3

creating safety

THE PRACTICE OF creating safety is based on the idea that the most important aspect of working with people is to build an environment that feels safe. When people feel safe, they take risks; they learn and try new things. A lot of lip service is given to concepts like risk and innovation, but rarely do work environments support them in action. When you focus on creating safety for yourself and others, work becomes easier to accomplish because more trust is created. If your workplace lacks trust, you can be part of the solution. Too often the blame is aimed at "them," but the truth is, as a leader, *it's up to you*.

Imagine This

Imagine you have just managed a large team to the finish line of a massive two-week push to release an important new piece of code. You are relatively new to the organization, and this was your first big project with the team. Working for the company has been your dream for many years. You can't believe that you are here and have just completed your first big initiative.

The goal was to finish the project by Friday, but, because of some unforeseen issues, it was not done until Sunday. Still, you feel proud that you, your team and your fellow colleagues put in the extra effort to make sure the code was ready before the start of the new business week. You all pulled off some long days and nights to meet the deadline. You are all exhausted and thrilled it is done. Your boss, John, has called a meeting. As you and the leadership group await him, the mood is light and celebratory. You are chatting and feel relieved the push for completion is over.

Then John enters the room. You can tell immediately that he is pissed off. The atmosphere shifts from one of celebration mixed with exhausted relief to an edgy stillness. John begins by saying how disappointed he is in the team. Obviously, he asserts, this leadership group and their respective teams don't care about deadlines or being a part of a world-class organization. If they did, they would have put forth whatever effort was needed to get the job done on time. John goes on to proclaim that from here on out he will be keeping tabs on each of them, looking for the weak links. Lack of attention to detail and missing timelines will not be tolerated.

John then singles out Charrise, the project lead. Focusing in on her, he declares she will take the brunt of the blame for the group's failure to deliver on time. He holds her responsible for the lack of discipline to "make it happen." By the end of the day, he expects a full accounting, indicating who shirked responsibility and who is to blame for missing the established timeline. With a stern, intimidating glare towards each of them, John picks up his things and leaves the room. You could hear a pin drop. You all stop breathing. Stunned, no one says a word.

John masterfully created a condition where no one felt safe. And while there was undoubtedly a lot happening in the scenario for everyone, the impact of this encounter is total erosion of trust on all fronts. Unfortunately, this is not an uncommon scenario. When trust is gone, you can bet productivity is going to be severely affected.

Better Safety

Use the "Imagine This" story to explore the topic of creating safety.

John, the boss

- What did he create in the room?
- What was he upset about?
- What might be causing that upset?
- How could he have addressed the situation so people felt safe?

_____

_____

Charrise, the project lead

- What was it like to be Charrise?
- What was she thinking?
- What was she feeling?
- How would you approach her situation?

_____

_____

You, a member of the leadership group .

- What was it like to be a member of the leadership group and a newcomer to the organization in that situation?
- What were you thinking?
- What were you feeling?
- How would you approach this situation to create more safety?

_____

_____

Connecting Trust and Productivity

Trust has a direct correlation to productivity. In his article "The Neuroscience of Trust," Paul J. Zak finds: "The effect of trust on self-reported work performance was powerful. Respondents whose companies were in the top quartile indicated they had 106% more energy and were 76% more engaged at work than respondents whose firms were in the bottom quartile. They also reported being 50% more productive."

Beyond the level of discretionary effort and drive that employees contribute in high-trust environments, there is an added benefit: these highly engaged employees plan to keep working with the organization. Zak's research found that trust profoundly impacts employee loyalty. "Compared with employees at low-trust companies, 50% more of those working at high-trust organizations planned to stay with their employer over the next year, and 88% more said they would recommend their company to family and friends as a place to work."[1]

We all know turnover is expensive. The Work Institute's *2019 Retention Report* estimates the cost of voluntary turnover in the United States during 2018 was $617 billion, as 41.4 million US employees quit their jobs.[2] In addition to being expensive, turnover creates tremendous disruption to internal teams and customers.

Trust is a key ingredient in productivity. Like us, you probably have a few books on your shelf that speak to this topic. Yet trust is one of the most elusive concepts out there. Amazon reports more than 6,000 books written about it. Many speak to the outcomes trust can produce and the indicators that help you know if it is present. Just about every company's value statement references trust, and it is a value held sacred in most relationships.

But what makes trust so important, especially to productivity? The presence of trust cements relationships by allowing people to feel safe; it fosters a sense of belonging to the group. When this happens, you bring more of yourself to the relationship. You are safe to be yourself without guarded filters. You are accepted for who you are. This sense of belonging promotes fully expressed individuals, aware of who they are and what they have to contribute.

Trust is a singular word with the power to influence so much. And words are like code. A word might mean one thing to you and something slightly different to someone else. This happens all the time—two people have a conversation, but they each experience and take away entirely different things from the exchange.

Kate and her former colleague Athena were co-facilitating a leadership development program with a cohort of people, mostly engineers from a Silicon Valley technology firm. As the morning session kicked off, you could feel the tension in the room. The participants were placating the facilitators, trying to do what was being asked, but the energy in the room was stalled. Folks were not engaging. Kate finally asked, "What is going on? You are all here but something else is present, something that is not being said. What is it?" A long, halting pause followed. Then, one brave soul spoke up: "We don't trust each other."

Aha! Without hesitating, Kate drew an imaginary line down the middle of the room, then directed, "Get up. Stand on this side of the room if you are the kind of person who trusts people implicitly—you trust people from the start. Stand on the other side of the room if people have to earn your trust—you trust only after a person demonstrates to you that they are trustworthy." People got up and stood on either side of the line.

With the group distributed between the two approaches to trust, Kate and Athena stimulated a dialogue about trust and how the group thought about it. The group got curious about what words meant to others in the room. They began to clear

Trust is a
singular word
**with the power
to influence
so much.**

out some old assumptions and create new actions that would deepen their connections with one another and allow relationships to move forward. Some committed to pausing rather than jumping to conclusions, seeking to understand where someone is coming from rather than making it up; and everyone began to see the value in leading with positive intentions.

The big takeaway: participants were shocked to realize how differently they each thought about trust, and how much their assumptions about other people got in the way of working well together. Their perceptions and underlying assumptions were creating roadblocks in their relationships that had stalled the productivity of this organization. We cannot recall the agenda for that morning, but what we do know is the most important work of the day took place. For at least one person, enough safety existed for him to boldly bring forward what needed to be addressed. That one person ignited a huge breakthrough in this cohort and for the organization.

Implicit and Earned Trust

Your perception of trust is powerful and it influences your behavior. Let's take a look at some of the various forms of trust and what is meant by them. Our reference point comes from the work of Robert Solomon and Fernando Flores, who suggest there are four types of trust.[3]

There is simple trust, such as the type of trust found in a healthy relationship between a parent and child. Unchallenged and untested, you might feel this way on your first day of school or when starting a new job—trusting the organization will set you up with the tools, information and insights you need to be successful. Simple trust is often taken for granted and exists unnoticed until it is lost.

Blind trust is the type of trust you put in an airplane pilot. Your faith is in an airline that has demonstrated a level of reliability and trustworthiness. And by extension, you trust their decisions to hire and train qualified pilots. Trust in leadership, where your need to believe in them creates a sense of safety and security, can be a form of blind trust. A factor of blind trust is a reluctance to experience the doubt or anxiety of distrust. You see only what you need to see and refuse to look, ask questions or truly comprehend what your senses might be telling you.

Conditional trust you might experience in the early days of a new job. At this stage, you are taking in so much information and meeting so many new people. As information comes in, you filter it, growing trust in others when the experience is a good one. When experiences are unpleasant or leave you feeling wary, questions arise along with doubt and suspicion. In reality, most trust becomes conditional, existing within specific boundaries or parameters where you feel safe.

Authentic trust could be reflected in the relationship you have with your favorite co-worker or best friend. Real experiences and interactions anchor this form of trust, interactions that have a history of repetition, dependability and predictably over time. These relationships are dynamic and filled with open, honest, unguarded interactions. Each person understands the trust boundaries and operates within them.

Another perspective on trust comes from Richard Fagerlin, founder and president of Peak Solutions, who claims, "Trust isn't something you earn, it's something that you give."[4] The issue with earned trust, he asserts, is that until trust is earned, you withhold it to protect yourself. The protective act limits your ability to trust. At the company level, that shows up as oppressive and defensive policies, overt micromanagement to maintain control and highly volatile reactions when dealing with uncertainty and conflict. When people act this way with one another, it's challenging to trust anyone—the result is people who do not trust, period.

Trust is reinforced through the consistency and predictability of words and actions. High trust is present when you know you are physically safe in this place and psychologically safe with these people.

Fagerlin places the obligation for creating trust squarely in your hands:

> Trust is the responsibility of the person who wants high trust. If you want others to trust you—it's your responsibility... If you are committed to giving and building trust, and determined to overcome any obstacles that stand in your way, you will win high trust. If you work patiently and with perseverance to lead your team towards a high-trust, high-performance culture, you can see it happen. Ten of the most powerful two-letter words in the English language are: *If it is to be, it is up to me.* If you are to have high trust in your relationships, it starts and ends with you.[5]

Trust is present when your people take risks and venture to learn new things. Trust is present when failure is a place to learn and challenging the status quo is valued because it helps everyone grow. In a healthy workplace culture, high levels of trust are evident, which allows you to bring the fullest expression of your potential to the workplace. You thrive, others thrive and the business thrives.

Creating Safety in the Workplace

Creating safety is the foundational practice that builds trust. Safety is a fork with two prongs: physical safety and psychological safety. Both are rooted in a value of caring for people.

When you care, you genuinely want to ensure the well-being of another. When a company is built with a community of people who genuinely care for one another, a culture of commitment is created. Commitment is the framework that lets people hold each other to high principles, to appreciate and respect each other, to challenge and encourage each other. And when people feel they are in a place that cares for them, it's reciprocated; you care for others, knowing you, too, are cared for. You feel safe.

Amy Edmondson, known for her pioneering work on psychological safety, notes that in the workplace, "[Psychological safety] is not the norm at all. In fact, I think it's unusual, which is what makes it potentially a competitive advantage. The reason why psychological safety is rare has to do with aspects of human nature, human instinct... For example, it is an instinct to want to look good in front of others. It's an instinct to divert blame... it's an instinct to agree with the boss. And hierarchies are places where these instincts are even more exaggerated."[6]

Nowhere were hierarchical instincts more exposed than in was what reported to have happened at Away. Away was founded in 2015 and labeled itself as a travel company. Its popular luggage piece "the Carry-On" first shipped in February 2016. And its rocket ship of success took off. In its first fiscal year the company sold $12 million in luggage, and by May 2018 the company had grown to more than 150 employees and achieved a valuation of $1.4 billion. The brand, popular with millennials, was recognized by *Adweek* as a "Breakthrough Brand with Ingenious Marketing," and accolades poured in from the likes of *Fast Company*, which recognized Away among the "2018 Top 10 Most Innovative Companies."[7]

But things changed on December 5, 2019, when technology website the Verge published the bombshell article "Emotional Baggage," which went viral.[8] This investigation, as reported by writer Zoe Schiffer, tells an all-too-common tale of a company whose narrative of caring for people was horrifically

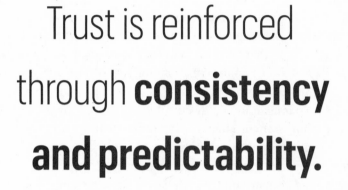

Trust is reinforced through **consistency and predictability.**

mismatched with its actions. The article describes painful details of a company culture that, despite promising a lifestyle of inclusion, was one of intimidation and bullying fueled by the behavior of its CEO and other leaders who masked their tirades in company values. It is a tale in which the desire for a culture of commitment to support the company's meteoric growth was co-opted by one of manipulated compliance. The Verge report has been vehemently disputed by Away and its CEO.[9] Regardless of the story's accuracy, we can look at the toxic culture examples to inform the importance of psychological safety at work.

One example shared reports of "Slack bullying." In the name of transparency, the article states, rules had been put into place so that nearly all communication took place digitally on Slack, an online collaboration app. Slack is a tool used in companies so people can ask questions, share updates and help one another stay current with what is happening—everything from product updates to welcoming new people or sharing good spots to eat in the neighborhood. It is a format for communicating that is more open than email, where access to a message is more limited. In theory, Slack can help promote open communications, and ideally it can be a positive culture move for an organization. But when Slack is used by colleagues and even top leaders to tear into people on public channels, this collaborative tool becomes toxic.

All that is good can equally be used for evil, or as mystery writer Harlan Coben has said, "I like to see the difference between good and evil as kind of like the foul line at a baseball game. It's very thin, it's made of something flimsy like lime, and if you cross it, it really starts to blur where fair becomes foul and foul becomes fair."[10] If you search "toxic culture" online, numerous examples pop up of company cultures driven by manipulation, coercion and bullying. None of these things creates a sense of safety or trust. They are perfect examples of leadership that makes producing results more important than the people creating those results. This approach produces cultures void of care, where people are relentlessly treated as resources, not humans.

When you feel unsafe

When you feel unsafe, hormones released from your sympathetic nervous system into your body signal an activation: the fight-flight-freeze response, or the infamous "amygdala hijack." The amygdala, which is part of the limbic system, is known for its role in the processing of fear and other emotions. These hormones tell you to stay and fight, freeze in place or flee. The response was designed to help humans survive stressful or life-threating situations. Without consciously doing anything, your body assesses each situation and determines which option will most likely help you survive a traumatic event. This response system helped our ancient ancestors survive when danger was all around.

Thankfully today, most workplaces, even at their worst, are not life-threating. Even so, the human nervous system has not fully evolved, and our bodies can trigger the fight-flight-freeze response when a situation is nonthreatening to survival—like speaking in front of a big audience, asking for a promotion or sharing bad news with your boss. These situations are not truly dangerous, but because they trigger your stress response, you react as if they were.

What happens for you in circumstances when you do not feel safe, either physically or psychologically? In chapter 2, we introduced you to compliers, protectors and controllers. Here we examine how these reactive tendencies align with the fight-flight-freeze response, and the impact of perceived threats on your sense of safety and well-being.

- **Freeze: the fear of not being good enough** (hello, compliers). This tendency is that little voice within you saying you're really not good enough and that what others think is more important. It ignites self-doubt and robs your ability to feel capable and competent to advocate for yourself or for others. Instead, you feel powerless and frozen.

- **Flight: the fear of not knowing** (hello, protectors). This is a little voice within you saying something here is not right, and not knowing feels dangerous. This response triggers you to withdraw and create distance. In some cases, the distance is physical; it can also appear as mental detachment or emotional aloofness, making you unavailable to create safety for yourself or others. You leave the room: mentally, emotionally and sometimes physically; you flee.

- **Fight: the fear of failure** (hello, controllers). The vise grip of this response is the fear of failure—the distress that you will let others or yourself down, that you will lose. You hate losing. You fight to rationalize that if you work harder, you can do more, be more, accomplish more; you will not disappoint yourself or others who depend on you. You want to win, at any cost. You focus all your energy on not failing.

A funny thing about reactive tendencies is that when one person in a room begins to react, it can create a domino effect: the controller proclaims that things weren't done the right way, which causes the compliers to think they aren't good enough and the protectors to point out all the errors in the controller's approach as they back away thinking, "Good luck with that!" Versions of this scenario are probably all too familiar. You have likely experienced first-hand how reactive tendencies coupled with fight-flight-freeze responses can stall the productive momentum of teams in the workplace.

Google is a company known for studying work habits inside the organization, especially the habits that transform productivity. To better understand the elements of great teamwork and what makes some teams thrive and others fail, Google initiated Project Aristotle, exploring the characteristics of its most successful teams. Researchers began the study with an assumption that building the best teams meant combining the best people. But no matter how they looked at it, they couldn't find a pattern there. They looked at 180 teams across the company but "the 'who' part of the equation didn't seem to matter," said Abeer Dubey, a manager in Google's People Analytics division, in a *New York Times Magazine* article by Charles Duhigg.[11] Julia Rozovsky, one of the lead researchers on the project, and her colleagues then looked more deeply into what group norms their most successful teams shared. This is where psychological safety stood out. As Duhigg notes:

> What Project Aristotle has taught people within Google is that no one wants to put on a "work face" when they get to the office. No one wants to leave part of their personality and inner life at home. But to be fully present at work, to feel "psychologically safe," we must know that we can be free enough, sometimes, to share the things that scare us without fear of recriminations. We must be able to talk about what is messy or sad, to have hard conversations with colleagues who are driving us crazy. We can't be focused just on efficiency. Rather, when we start the morning by collaborating with a team of engineers and then send emails to our marketing colleagues and then jump on a conference call, we want to know that those people really hear us. We want to know that work is more than just labor.[12]

Of the key dynamics that set successful teams apart from other teams at Google, the data indicated that psychological safety, more than anything else, is critical to making a team work.

Trust begins with you

We tend to deflect responsibility for making things better to "them." But the truth is, a committed, caring culture is the responsibility of every person who is part of the community. You are responsible for creating safety in your workplace. Whether you are in the C-suite, a manager or an individual contributor—safety begins with you. Henry Kimsey-House, one of the founders of professional coaching and the Co-Active Training Institute, said to us once that he does not believe we can change an organization. Rather, we can change this person and this person and this person. Each begins to change how the organization functions. You are part of the solution. *It's up to you* to create a healthy workplace culture where people feel safe and trust is reflected in each person's actions.

In the article "The Essential Importance of Trust: How to Build It or Restore It," Dennis Jaffe notes one definition of trust is "feeling safe when vulnerable."[13] Showing care for the people around you is that first act of vulnerability. Like the brave soul in our leadership training session who spoke up about the lack of trust in the room, when you change your actions, you pave the way for others to participate. Commit to creating more safety and more trust, for you and for those in your organization. If you take a stand for it, you will influence the people around you.

Ryan Merkley, the chief of staff at Wikimedia Foundation (the nonprofit that hosts Wikipedia), was a fixer, someone who goes into the burning building and puts out fires. He says that as a leader, he was very effective at getting things done and getting teams to deliver, but fixing problems can also create challenges for working relationships. When Ryan participated in the Five Practices training, he went through "the most transformative leadership experience" he has ever had, and it completely changed the way he leads. He looked at the question "How does trust affect a company?" and realized that his team "needs to know [he] care[s] about them." Today, he builds his leadership around trust. He says, at Wikimedia, they live by these mottos:

- "Everyone makes it across the river together."
- "Collaboration moves at the speed of trust."
- "Show your work, show your heart."

Statements that have allowed the Wikimedia teams to flourish.[14]

Core Skill: Listening

The first step towards caring about people and creating safety is to know what is needed and to bring it. Become the person seeking to understand what is happening, and from that place, discern what is needed to generate forward momentum. A great skill for this is listening. It is so basic, and that's the beauty of it. No special equipment needed.

Expanding how you listen and what you do with what you hear are essential steps to creating safety. By listening, you come to understand another human. Listening lets people know that their thoughts and ideas matter, and that both they and their ideas are important and respected. It tells people they have been seen and heard, and it is a key skill to unlocking misunderstandings and tensions. Listening enhances collaboration and supports connection with the humans you work with. It is the gateway to understanding.

You may be familiar with active listening, a technique of observing a speaker's behavior and body language for a more accurate understanding of what they are trying to

Listening lets people know that their thoughts and ideas matter, and that both they and their ideas are important and respected.

communicate. You validate what you think you heard by para-phrasing back to the speaker. This super-helpful technique can benefit some situations. However, not all situations are created equal, and a singular approach has its limitations. At HumanityWorks, we use a model that we first learned from the Co-Active Training Institute called Three Levels of Listen-ing.[15] This model helps you become more conscious of how you listen. It also provides techniques that help you under-stand what is being communicated and how to discern what is needed. A foundational skill, using the three levels of listening is a stronghold for creating safety.

Level 1: Internal listening

At level 1, your awareness is on you. You listen to the words of the other person, but your attention is on what those words mean to you. Using a hypothetical example from the work-place, imagine you are giving your CEO a weekly update in a face-to-face meeting. She looks irritated and begins frantically typing something into her phone. You are sitting right in front of her, in the middle of your update, and you begin to wonder if she is sending you feedback via Slack.

At this point you begin listening to the voice inside your head. Clearly (in your mind) you did something to annoy her. You start arming your defensive position for why you did what-ever you did that apparently irritated her. You create a list of all the things you might have unknowingly said that triggered her ire. You might be feeling annoyed by her dismissive behavior and notice your own ire rising. These are examples of level 1 listening, the spotlight is on "me": my thoughts, my judgments, my feelings, my opinions, my anxiety and my conclusions.

The value of level 1 listening

In the spirit of creating safety, level 1 listening helps you iden-tify when things don't feel safe *for you*.

Level 1 listening is where your intuition lives—we think intuition is among the highest forms of intelligence. Intuition is your brain gathering and processing facts—many happening outside your awareness—and forming them into patterns. These are sent to your high-brain processing areas. That "gut feeling" you get is literally neurons in your digestive system signaling a pattern match. Take note and listen when you feel the flutter of butterflies or that queasy, uneasy feeling. That's your intuition speaking to you.

Level 1 listening connects you to what matters to you. Becoming aware of your level 1 reactions allows you to consider what you do or do not like about your experience. It broadens the questions you ask of yourself, and it can clarify your next action. "How does this relate to me? What is interesting about this to me?"

This level of listening helps you make sense of your experience. It is a place to question what is happening and notice how you feel about it. Connecting in this way helps you understand your reactions. It also creates a pause during which you can question what is happening around you. Values are ignited in level 1; they rest just under the surface of your consciousness and are triggered when things around you just don't seem "right." Happy, positive experiences may also trigger your values.

When you are triggered, pause. The pause will help deepen awareness of your values—knowing what really matters to you and why will aim your actions going forward in more meaningful, impactful ways.

Listening tips, level 1

Believe it or not, it is not all about you all the time. Level 1 is the "me" channel, and it can be limiting to hang out here too much or for too long. Thus, we offer a warning label to level 1 listening. Listening at this level pulls your focus away from other people. It limits your ability to be present with others and constricts awareness of your surroundings. When listening in level 1, you can become overly focused on your own internal dialogue and miss the opportunity to create a caring connection. Here are some warning signs you might be stuck on the "me" channel:

- You spend more time preparing your response than you do listening to what is being said.

- You find your own soundtrack more interesting than what others are saying.

- You stop listening and are dismissive of the speaker because you don't like what they are saying.

- You become intolerant of what is being said and cut the other speaker off before they are done.

- You are busy configuring a reply to match or top the speaker's experience.

If you notice any of these things happening, it is a signal that a different level of listening will offer more information about what is happening.

Level 2: Focused listening

In level 2 listening, you focus intently on the other person. Think about being out with a great friend. They are telling you about something that recently happened to them, and you are enthralled. Maybe it was something that happened on vacation or at work, or a casual encounter at the pet store—the topic doesn't matter. What does matter is all your attention and curiosity concentrates on them and their experience. We sometimes describe this as the level of attention you give to someone when you are first falling in love. You are fascinated with everything they have to share with you.

Listening in level 2 takes discipline and self-management. In the "Imagine This" scenario of John, the upset, disappointed boss, applying level 2 listening with him would mean a hard focus on listening to what is happening for him. The trick to listening at level 2 is to avoid judgment—and the antidote for that is curiosity.

Get *curious* about what he is doing and why he is doing it, without judgment or assumptions. Listen to his choice of words, to what he's saying and what he might be trying to convey, where he feels challenged or constrained. At level 2, you become an observer of human behavior, noticing what is said and how it is said. Notice his emotions: What are they about? What is he afraid of? Something did not feel safe to him. Listening in this way helps you unearth it.

The value of level 2 listening

When you listen at level 2, you are creating safety for the other person. You show they are cared for. Listening in such a present and attentive manner helps them feel seen—sometimes for the first time. All your curiosity is about them and their experience. Ask questions like: "And then what happened?" "And then what did you do?" As you deepen the conversation, ask, "What is important for you about this?"

At level 2, you demonstrate that what another person has to say is important. It is a form of witnessing. You acknowledge their experience and its meaning. You might ask: "What does this mean to you?" "What do you need or want?" "What would serve you best right now?"

You also validate that they are valued. Level 2 listening teaches you so much about the other person. Being heard helps people feel understood. This is a powerful expression of care and respect for another human. Deepen your caring connection with questions like: "What was significant about that?" "What was that like for you?" "What's it like to be misunderstood?"

Listening tips, level 2

While the benefits of level 2 listening are tremendous for establishing caring connections and creating safety, it takes energy to stay focused on another human in such an intense way. These tips help you care for yourself so you can continue to care for others:

- Regulate your listening. Check in with each other before jumping in. Ask your conversation partner, "What will serve you best right now?"

- Put aside what you know, momentarily. Hold space for the other person's discovery.

- Practice the art of managing your own reactions and ideas. It's up to you to be patient, to stay when it gets hard, to not fix it or make it okay when it gets messy. You are right where you need to be. You've got this.

- Be generous with your self-care. Level 2 listening can be intense in its highs and in its lows. You may need time to recover after witnessing others in such an intense and focused way. Find out what works for you.

Level 3: Global listening

Level 3 listening is sometimes described as environmental listening or global listening. It is the ability to read a room—the mood, the emotions, the unspoken information—and monitor how it changes in response to what is happening in the space. Comedians, musicians, trainers and actors all have this ability.

It includes observing the action, the inaction and the interaction in a group.

Think about the example that we began the chapter with: Your boss walks into the room and you can tell he is annoyed. Immediately the energy in the room shifts from one of exhausted relief to being on edge. You may not know the context of his annoyance, but you know bad news is coming. Noticing body language, eye contact or lack of it, what people are saying or not saying, are all elements of level 3 listening.

Listening at level 3 requires you to take in available information in a different format. Think about sitting at the conference table when everyone becomes silent in the opening story. What unspoken information is communicated? What was the body language of the team as the boss ranted on? Where were eyes looking? What happened when the boss zeroed in on Charrise? How did the air feel? Other than words, what were you hearing?

The information is there for you to mine, simply by tuning in and being aware that it is there. When creating safety, level 3 listening offers vital clues, sometimes communicated silently, to what is needed—and it's up to you to give it voice.

The value of level 3 listening

When listening at level 3, you have the opportunity to create safety for yourself and others by giving voice to what is not being said. You expose what is going on underneath the surface, without having to fix it. If you sense confusion, you might voice: "What are we solving for?" If you encounter gridlock, you can ask, "What are people not saying that needs to be said?" You reveal the elephant in the room so it can be addressed. The level 3 could be tension, or it could be frustration because folks are dodging the real issue at hand. You might question: "What are we trying to accomplish?" or "What are we tolerating that no longer serves us?"

At level 3 listening, you acknowledge that emotion is present so it can be moved past. When folks pick up situations that feel "charged" or messy, many tend to avoid these emotions. Ironically, that's when acknowledging it can help you put it down. Just naming it can create more safety in the room. You state what is present: "It's clear people have a lot of passion about this topic. What's important here?" "I can feel how intense the emotions are. What's needed now?" or "What is not needed now?"

You create a path to a bigger conversation. If the level 3 feels excited, energetic, wandering, maybe even confused, naming it makes it safe to not know. Stating what you pick up with level 3 listening could sound like: "What do we want?" or "What will that get us?" and "Where can that lead?" You are creating safety for folks to imagine what could be.

You also move people into action. When intense emotions arise, people can become literally frozen in place, especially if there is discomfort, fear, agitation... you get the idea. You can unlock the room by stating what is present: "People are uncomfortable and may not feel safe to say what they are really thinking." You create safety by taking a stand for those who, at that moment, cannot speak for themselves.

Listening tips, level 3

You can develop techniques to support level 3 listening:

- **Pause:** When you speak to level 3 in the room, it can create a powerful pause, giving everyone a chance to regroup. This gives you a heartbeat to assess what is happening now and what might be needed next.

- **Take courage:** Giving voice to what is present in level 3 can be vulnerable work. Showing care for the people around you is the first act of vulnerability, and it shows the way for others.

- **Be approachable:** Pay attention to *how* you give voice to what you sense at level 3. Avoid statements of judgment, shame or blame. You want everyone in the room to feel safe to participate, so let the best of your emotions fuel your courage to act and to create the outcome you want.

- **Trust yourself:** Information is available in level 3, if you allow yourself to go there. Observe the mood of the group. Try to name the energy in the room: Is it sleepy? On edge? Waiting? Anxious? Based on what you discover, what is needed? Ask questions to ignite that!

Creating Safety through Listening

One of our favorite examples of creating safety through listening is from the CEO of an early-stage start-up where Debbie spent a day while she was being recruited. This particular day was a Friday, the day the company held its weekly "all-hands" meeting. Everyone in the company came together to get clear information and align on areas of common interest. What was memorable about this visit was the CEO's opening ritual.

She began each all-hands meeting with the same game. She breezed in and stood at the front of the room, pulling a raggedy scrap of paper from her back pocket. "Truths and Lies," she announced. The room stilled. "First, rumor has it I am going to be throwing out the first pitch at the Giants game on Sunday." The room erupted with cries of "truth, truth!" or "lies, it's a lie!" She smiled and let the energy run its course. Then she admitted, "Not true. I will not be throwing out the opening pitch. Still on my bucket list."

Next, a rumor circulating the halls: "A hedge fund is about to buy us, and everyone is going to lose their jobs." The room responded with boos and a sea of thumbs-downs. She laughed and quickly quelled that rumor as "not true." And finally, watercooler chatter: "We have secured our next round of funding." Again, the room broke into chants of "truth!" When the crowd died down, she admitted (to clapping and cheers) that they had, indeed, secured the next round of funding, and she invited the CFO to take the team through the details and what to expect in the near-term.

It's noteworthy that she mined her weekly agenda from the needs of her people. Watercooler talk can so quickly turn into rumor and speculation, igniting political divides and diverting people's attention from the important tasks at hand. When topics are left unaddressed, they turn into pettiness and gossip. This CEO hit it head-on. She didn't lead with her agenda, she started with theirs—and bonus points for keeping it fun. Her approach ingrained a sense of trustworthiness within the culture. She cared for her people. One way she expressed the depth of this care was to be forthright and truthful, to listen to their concerns, big and small, and dispel concerns, speculation or rumors. In this workplace, it was safe to be curious, ask questions and be truthful.

This CEO's recipe had a few ingredients for success that leaders might take note of. One was how she mined the organization for information. Her insights were gained though level 2 (hard focus on others) and level 3 (sensing the energy) listening. She walked the halls, curious about what was on the minds of her people. She sought to understand what was happening for them, what they were concerned about, what was getting in their way. The time she invested in fostering meaningful connections helped create a sense of safety, a place people felt cared for, and a shared sense of what could be possible for this early-stage start-up.

It is not always so rosy. In the story above, folks were willing to share what was on their mind. Sometimes your people are silent. Sometimes they are not forthcoming about what they are thinking or feeling. There is information there too. Silence can be a signal that they do not feel safe. It's up to you to get curious, to listen deeply at levels 1, 2 and 3.

All three levels of listening are needed. They are powerful tools to create safety. The art of listening is not to stay in *any one* of these levels. You want to develop the ability to move with agility between *all three* levels, mining for information. What is each level telling you? Effective listening happens when you scan each of the levels for information.

Listening is a powerful skill with application in all of our practices. It is offered as part of creating safety because it is an essential skill to generate the depth of caring connections people need to feel physically and psychologically safe with one another. It is a building block of trust.

Mindset Shift: Boundaries

As we established in chapter 2, real growth that changes behavior requires more than applying a newly learned skill. That skill needs to be applied to a new way of thinking about the world—a shift in your mindset. The mindset shift we're inviting you to play with for creating safety is around boundaries, which are used to let people in, rather than keep people out. They provide a clarity for you and for others about what is and is not okay.

We use the three levels of listening to discern "What am I okay with and what am I not okay with?" This will shift you from not knowing what to do in a situation that feels unsafe to deciding how to create the safety you and others need.

We were leading session three of a five-part leadership development program. The design brings a cohort of folks from one organization together for ten days over seven months.

**Listening generates
the depth of caring
connection people need**
to feel safe with one another.
It is a building block of trust.

The span and duration provide the cohort time to build skills and strengthen trusting relationships with one another. We have found it to be a successful, high-leverage approach to up-level emerging leaders and to ignite deep change within an organization. The structure of the cohort had very clearly stated boundaries established by our client. One was you cannot miss a session and still be in the cohort. Tough, we know. The structure existed for a purpose; the ground rules are clearly communicated with participants before they commit. This hard boundary creates strong commitments: to the learning process, to each other and to the journey they are going through *together*. By the third session, the cohort has formed tight bonds.

As the day began, everyone noticed one person was missing. The level 3 impact on the room was palpable. Folks were unsettled, distracted, unfocused. An assistant in the back of the room was asked to check in on the person and report back. The room needed to know that the person we all cared about was okay, that they were safe. With that action in motion, the room settled, the group began to focus, and the program could begin.

At the lunch break, Debbie was called away. The missing participant was outside and wanted to speak with her. It turns out this person had spent the night in jail, having been arrested on the way to the retreat. Remorseful, tearful, this person asked to return to the group.

As facilitators who were responsible for the safety and well-being of the whole group, we discussed this turn of events and decided to deny the request. Our rationale was three-fold and correlated to the three levels of listening.

Level 1—The "me" channel, where intuition and values live

We had to check in with ourselves: What were our own level 1s telling us? What were we okay with and what were we not okay with? A bit of wrestling took place between our hearts and our heads. Ultimately, our level 1 listening landed on the participation boundary set for the group. It was in place so participants would commit to quieting external stimuli and focusing on themselves, being present to the concepts and their interactions—to commit to the growth and evolution that was taking place for themselves and for the cohort. We needed to honor that boundary.

Level 2—The hard focus on the other, using curiosity to quiet judgment

In this case, we had two "others" to consider. One was the person who was in this challenging circumstance. With them, Debbie was full heart-forward listening to what they had to say and being with the pain they were experiencing without feeling like she had to solve it. Debbie's goal was to stay curious with them about the circumstance and what they were taking from it.

Additionally, we had a room full of "others" who deeply cared about this person. Listening at level 2, we asked: "What would serve them?" "What are they showing us that they need?" "What are we hearing that tells us the needs of everyone can be met by holding to the agreed-upon boundaries?"

There were different needs to be honored at level 2. They needed to know their colleague was safe and cared for, and that if something unforetold happened to any of them, they would also be treated in a fair and compassionate way. And this participant had some big issues that could no longer be ignored or stepped over.

Level 3—Mining the space for unspoken information

We mined level 3 for what the cohort needed. Had the group moved on? What was in their level 3 concerning the absence of this participant?

Our own level 3 listening kept aiming towards the old saying that you cannot stand in the same river twice. One reason the boundary existed is that a lot happens in the room in a short span of time. The cohort had had significant experiences together during the course of the morning. It was different now than it had been five hours before; the group had moved forward without their colleague. Introducing the colleague back into the cohort would have set back the momentum of the group.

Better Listening

Imagine yourself as a facilitator in the retreat scenario:

- What would your level 1 listening be telling you about what was going on for you?
- What would your level 2 listening be telling you about both the individual and the rest of the group?
- What would your level 3 listening be telling you about what was unspoken?

_____

_____

_____

_____

_____

_____

Holding a Boundary with Love

It was a tough decision and a tough message to deliver to the individual and to the cohort.

The individual felt very safe with Debbie and was open and candid about their personal circumstance. They were in a tough spot, a pivotal decision point *in their life*. They had a lot of things to work through. And to deeply change as they professed to want, they would need the same type of commitment that this leadership development program required. That work needed to happen with the supportive presence of professionals with a different set of expertise. This was a hard, tough-love kind of conversation between Debbie and the person, where we asserted the boundary as a focus on commitment—to themself. This person went away and did some big, important work. They joined the next cohort and have since gone on to do great things in their life and for the company.

With the cohort, our role was to facilitate a conversation so they could derive meaning from the circumstance safely, so that everyone could continue on the journey, gleaning insight from this experience into their own growth as a leader. As a leader, it's important to ensure that the needs of the whole are not overtaken by the needs of an individual. Your role is to make it safe for all members of your group. The mindset you hold about boundaries becomes a key factor in this.

As a duo, this was a hard one. We really cared (and still care) about this person. They were in pain and made a request that we had the power to simply say yes to. We could have relaxed the boundary, but in this case, the easy thing would not have been the right thing to do for any of those involved. It was helpful to have each other to do this hard work with.

We held on to a higher objective—that the boundary was not keeping this person out. It let them, and the cohort, into a deeper understanding of themselves and the significant change that can occur when you commit. The group was disappointed but understood, and we could move forward. We modeled for the group how to hold a boundary with, dare we say it, love and respect for all involved, and this created safety.

4

working together

THE PRACTICE OF working together is based on the belief that true collaboration yields an abundance of creativity, brilliance and magic—much more so than doing something on your own. Better ideas and solutions come when you seek to understand others and the roots of your own perspective. The "other" in the equation might be people in your meeting, on your team, in your training program—or a peer, boss, client or partner. Working together is the practice of being supportive and acknowledging them, being curious in the face of challenges and not being attached to your own point of view. It means being clear on your outcome, being open to how you can achieve it and having faith in the power of co-creating. When you can cultivate that, you are "in it" together. You come to know and trust more about one another, which in turn creates more resilience within a team and an organization. When working together, *it's not about you*, it's all about them.

Imagine This

The head of a technology group was deep in conversation with his HR business partner about a performance issue on their team. The employee, we will call him Jeff, had become unreliable, some days just not bothering to show up at work— no notice, no call, just ghosting. In the months preceding this conversation, there had been an ongoing escalation of performance-related issues linked back to Jeff's unreliability.

The manager felt like he had done all he could and was clearly fed up. He had brought issues up with Jeff as they were happening, told Jeff what needed to be done differently, and made his expectations clearly known. He was sure Jeff had heard his messages, only to face more backsliding in performance. The situation had not improved. In fact, the unreliable nature of Jeff's performance had become intolerable for the manager; Jeff's poor performance was affecting service to internal clients and creating an undue burden on the rest of the team. The manager had hit his limit of trying to work with Jeff and was ready to move him into a performance improvement plan (PIP). A PIP is, in reality, a final notice to improve or be terminated. Jeff would have two options: ongoing, sustained improvement or losing his job.

The severity of the issue caused the HR business partner, who reported to Debbie, to flag this circumstance for her review. Something about the scenario did not sit quite right with Debbie. Jeff had been a top performer, highly rated and highly regarded within the organization. He had been deeply engaged, a pivotal figure to employees and a cheerleader of the brand. His level of customer service had been exemplary. When Debbie first joined the company, Jeff went out of his way to pop by each evening and check in with her. Jeff would pull up a chair and chat about his day and his life, and provide important context about the company and culture, the kind that doesn't come in a handbook. He was friendly, helpful, outgoing.

Debbie met with the HR business partner, the manager and his boss for greater context and to make sure they knew their concerns were taken seriously. But one voice was still missing: Jeff's. Debbie called him and left a message. She let him know she was concerned about him, that she had learned he'd had unexplained absences and wanted to understand more. She instructed him to report to her office the following morning at a prescribed time so they could check in. And she let him know that just the two of them would be meeting, no manager.

The next morning Jeff appeared, as requested. Opening with a simple, heartfelt, "I'm concerned about you," Debbie then asked, "What's happening for you?" Jeff burst open like stop gates in a flood. The crux of it all: he was having severe mental health issues. Jeff had faced this kind of challenge before. On a recent visit home, his parents had recognized the signs and had gotten him help. But his condition was fragile. Each day brought unknown landmines and unidentified barriers. Some days were good, others not so much. Some days took unexpected detours. He felt bad about what was going on at work but had not felt secure talking to his manager about the issue.

Debbie and the HR business partner worked with Jeff and his manager to reach an outcome that met both of their needs: for Jeff to keep working in a limited way as a helpful structure that could support his health concerns, and for his manager to have reliable, dependable information about Jeff's capacity. Everyone was committed to helping Jeff return to work in a healthy, fully present and productive way.

People are humans, not resources. There are times when an employee needs to be put on a PIP. And there are times when folks reach for the policies and practices at their disposal and solve for the wrong problem. The expedient route could have been to put Jeff on a PIP. In that scenario, he would have failed within a week, a replacement would have been hired and the company would have moved on. That is the humans-are-resources scenario. And for Jeff, the outcome of that scenario would have been precarious. In this instance, seeking greater understanding of what was going on with that human being made the difference. With greater understanding, the team could appreciate the struggles being expressed and work together to improve the situation for all concerned.

This was not simple or easy. It took a lot of open, sincere communication to understand what everyone needed and to create, together, the best path forward. Clear boundaries and accountabilities were put into place for Jeff that were helpful to him and provided the company with some assurance that the current situation would not go on indefinitely.

In these hard and messy moments, it's so important to remember that it's not about you, it's about them. When you do this, you will find that acceptance lends depth to your interactions, breadth to your own understanding and richness to your relationships. This is true in the workplace and in all areas of life.

Connecting Resilience and Productivity

Resilience is the capacity to recover quickly from challenges. When resilience is present, people spring back from challenges with ease—a critical capability for productivity and business success. Creating resilient organizations is a human challenge, not just a workplace problem. On June 8, 2020, the World Bank released an article examining the economic impact of the COVID-19 pandemic in which it concludes, "Global coordination and cooperation... provide the greatest chance of achieving public health goals and enabling a robust global recovery."[1]

meQuilibrium studied resilience in a research project, interviewing more than 2,000 people ranging in age from eighteen to sixty-four. The study found that if employees are more resilient, they are more productive. "'The evidence is in: resilience has a measurable, proven effect on your bottom line,' said Jan Bruce, co-founder and CEO of meQuilibrium. 'Resilience isn't just a nice-to-have, but a foundational business imperative because having a happier, less stressed, more engaged and focused workforce delivers higher productivity, lower healthcare costs, less absenteeism—and better overall financial performance.'"[2]

Other studies have revealed that people with more resilience perform better and respond better to change. They are more motivated, build better working relationships and are less likely to be absent because of illness or suffer from low morale. They also have ways to buffer stress.[3]

Highlights of meQuilibrium's research include:

- **Stress:** Highly resilient employees exhibited 46 percent less stress than workers with low resilience.

- **Satisfaction:** Resilient employees were four times as satisfied with their jobs.

- **Attrition:** Low-resilience employees were twice as likely to quit.[4]

Fortune 100 companies like IBM, Shell, DuPont and Unilever have begun to focus on resilience as a strategic imperative, with focus on both business continuity and employee well-being. They understand the link between the resilience of their workforce and overall business productivity.

Working Together to Unleash the Magic

Working together democratizes information, expands knowledge transfer and increases workflow. Collaboration generates more creativity and innovation. Constructive collaboration improves team morale and increases engagement. You are inextricably linked to others. How you work together becomes key to being good humans and making work better. When leaders realize it no longer serves to focus solely on their own results, teams and companies become more resilient and more productive. We think of this dynamic equation as: You + Other = Amazing!

When groups begin to work together for the first time, it is a bit like blending families. Each unit comes to the new relationship with all kinds of history, rituals, war stories, policies, procedures and structures. These units then have to figure out what will be adopted, integrated or let go of and what new things will be created. Too often, a part of the journey overlooked in becoming one new company is honoring the past of each unit.

We were asked to help the leadership teams of two recently merged companies through this initial phase. Our challenge was to blend their two families into one so they could begin the new journey of working together.

After they'd had some time getting to know one another, we divided the teams into four groups. We gave each a wall-sized timeline graphic and a ton of arts and crafts materials for them to create a timeline featuring the significant high and low points of their history. There were no right or wrong ways to go about it. Some groups focused on business strategy and outcomes, shipping pieces of code or product launches. Others incorporated highlights of key people joining or low points of people departing the organization. They included big wins and disappointments. All expressed themselves with their own artistic flare. Then, each group shared their stories, helping those in the room understand more about their journey: what they cherished, what they were sad to leave behind and what they were excited to move towards.

When a group was presenting, the rest of the room was to bear witness. Sharing your story helps you be seen. And once you feel seen and understood, it's easier to acknowledge the

Equation for constructive collaboration:

You + Other = Amazing!

important parts of your past to carry forward and what no longer serves you. Out of a space to grieve what will no longer be and identify what remains important, something new can emerge, something different that serves this new point in time. The result for the merged teams was that barriers began to come down. It was the first time everyone was in the same room as leaders, being humans together, figuring out how to work together, with one shared goal. It was amazing.

Working together in a culture where candor and respectful disagreement is encouraged can have fantastic results. Ed Catmull, president of Pixar Animation Studios, realized how important this is. He tells the story of how Pixar established such a culture of candor and its impact on the creative process in his book, *Creativity, Inc.*[5] Pixar Animation Studios began in 1979 as part of the Lucasfilm computer division, before its spinoff as a corporation in 1986. Two decades later, in 2006, Disney purchased Pixar at a valuation of $7.4 billion. Over its history, Pixar has produced several dozen feature films, including *Toy Story*, *Ratatouille*, *Monsters, Inc.*, *Finding Nemo*, *WALL-E* and *Up*, each of which offers groundbreaking animation and audience appeal.

Catmull credits the success of the creative process to a culture of candor. "Why? Because early on, all of our movies suck. That's a blunt assessment, I know, but I choose that phrasing because saying it in a softer way fails to convey how bad the first versions really are. I'm not trying to be modest or self-effacing. Pixar films are not good at first, and our job is to make them so—to go, as I say, 'from suck to not-suck.'"[6] As Catmull says, "A hallmark of a healthy creative culture is that its people feel free to share ideas, opinions, and criticisms. Our decision making is better when we draw on the collective knowledge and unvarnished opinions of the group. Candor is the key to collaborating effectively. Lack of candor leads to dysfunctional environments."

The Braintrust was created as a safe structure for this type of candor to take place, and to signal its significance for Pixar's success. Functioning much like an academic peer review, the Braintrust is composed mostly of colleagues and peers who have expertise in and empathy for the creation, storytelling chops, and an understanding of how challenging the work is. Meeting every few months, the Braintrust assesses each movie being made. Catmull notes, "Its premise is simple: Put smart, passionate people in a room together, charge them with identifying and solving problems, and encourage them to be candid."[7] The Braintrust broadens the perspective of everyone involved on a film by peering "at least briefly, though others' eyes." As Catmull says, the Braintrust is "a forum that ensures we raise our game—not by being prescriptive but by offering candor and deep analysis... It's not foolproof... but when we get it right, the results are phenomenal."[8]

Pixar films have earned sixteen Academy Awards, ten Golden Globes and eleven Grammys, along with numerous other awards and recognitions. Also noteworthy is Pixar's impressive rating as a preferred place to work. As one employee review put it, "Pixar has time and time again put employees first, but also demanding excellence from everyone. The culture is alive, and the people are sincere and real. Our movies can attest to the deep-down emotions we are able to pull out on a daily basis and work through together."[9]

Not every workplace has a group like the Braintrust. But whenever you work with others, a moment will inevitably occur when someone offers thoughts on how you are doing something, and it will set you off. The feedback may come directly or indirectly, formally or informally, and it may leave you feeling a range of emotions: angry, anxious, misunderstood, maybe profoundly threatened. What's that all about?

Authors Sheila Heen and Douglas Stone offer a fresh perspective in their article "Find the Coaching in Criticism." When it comes to receiving feedback, they note, "the process strikes at the tension between two core human needs—the need to learn and grow, and the need to be accepted just the way you are ... Getting better at receiving feedback starts with understanding and managing those feelings." You might think there are a thousand ways that feedback could push your buttons, but Heen and Stone claim there are three: truth triggers, relationship triggers and identity triggers.

> *Truth triggers* are set off by the content of the feedback. When assessments or advice seems off base, unhelpful, or simply untrue, you feel indignant, wronged, and exasperated.

> *Relationship triggers* are tripped by the person providing the feedback. Exchanges are often influenced by what you believe about the giver (He's got no credibility on this topic!) and how you feel about your previous interactions (After all I've done for you, I get this petty criticism?). So you might reject input that you would accept on its merits if it came from someone else.

> *Identity triggers* are all about your relationship with yourself. Whether the feedback is right or wrong, wise or baseless, it can be devastating if it causes your sense of who you are to come undone. In such moments you'll struggle with feeling overwhelmed, defensive, or off balance.[10]

When you feel judged in some way and you are triggered (truth, relationship and/or identity), get curious about the feedback. The solution isn't to pretend you haven't been triggered. It's to notice and become inquisitive. What is your trigger signaling?

Core Skill: Perspective

Whereas your mindset is a habitual, embedded way of thinking, your perspective is a particular outlook or point of view you have about something. Just like a photographer chooses a lens to capture reality in different ways, we each have filters through which we see the world. These filters are part of past experience, race, culture, age, economic status, beliefs, fears, hopes, dreams and much more.

As you receive new information or have new experiences, your perspective can change. Sometimes perspectives change because something dramatic happens to you: someone close to you dies, you fall in love or you experience the wonder of traveling to another country. Sometimes perspective shifts are slower and they change with your life circumstances: views of politics, success, money, status and power. As you move through careers or change jobs or industries, your perspective about your relationship to work—including on what it's like to work with other people, manage others, be managed by someone younger (or older), lead a company or tell someone they are fired—may shift. Perspectives are fluid and you can be in choice about them. This gets tricky, though, because most of the time people are unconscious of even being in a perspective. To be able to identify the perspective you are in and consciously choose your perspective is a practice.

Your perspectives shape the way you think, decide and act. Often when you are in a perspective, you believe it is *the truth*, not just the way you personally view a situation or a person. This is where you need to get curious about your filters, about the lens through which you are seeing. Pause to unearth and examine your beliefs about the situation you face and see what comes up.

Better Perspective, Part 1

When it comes to working together with others, what perspectives do you tend to stand in?

- I know I have to work with others, but it always takes longer.
- I feel like when I am open to the ideas of others; we always come up with more creative solutions.
- I like working with others, except sometimes I feel like my voice gets lost.
- I know I have to work with other people, but it can get hard when emotions get in the way.
- I feel like other people are just getting in the way of what I need to get done.
- I like working with other people on projects; it's more fun than working by myself.
- I like working with other people because I always learn so much.

What other statements might capture your default perspectives?

_____

_____

_____

_____

_____

_____

_____

_____

Examining your feelings and assumptions

It's imperative to examine your feelings and assumptions about working together with others. You can be fully aware of your feelings, and you should be. However, when you stand firmly entrenched in a perspective, unwilling to be open to others' views, you become an impediment to working together and a roadblock to manifesting resilience in your workplace.

When you are in a perspective about working together with someone, get curious about how you see the situation or the person. For example, perhaps you believe that a certain person is difficult to work with. Is that the absolute truth? Or did you hear it from others? Or was that person going through something difficult the last time you worked with them? Experiment with holding a different perspective, such as "When I can find common ground, I can easily work with anyone" or "She is passionate about her work and I appreciate that passion" or "I'm curious about him and how to work best with him."

Debbie worked with a client, a newly promoted female VP of a product group, who expressed frustration that her male counterpart approached the work from the attitude of "winner takes all." She was trapped in this perspective and the success of the project was at risk. Her view that he wanted to "win" created the assumption that she then had to "lose." This perspective limited their respective teams, which were dependent on each other to achieve a mutual goal. The teams needed each other and they needed to work together. But the perspectives and related actions of the two leaders strained the groups and, therefore, neither was being successful. They were pulling away from each other and had lost sight of the common goal. To "win" was about the successful completion of the project. To "win" required both teams to work together. Instead, the tension between the teams had stalled all forward momentum.

During a coaching session, Debbie used an analogy of a rubber band: Envision your hands together with one rubber band around the outside of them. Now pull them apart as far as you can. As your hands stretch apart, you create tension on the rubber band. In this analogy, people are the hands and the rubber band represents your common goal. There are two outcomes: the hands can either continue to separate and eventually snap the rubber band, or the hands can come together and relieve the tension. Now ask yourself: "What does coming together look like?" and "What is at risk if they do not come together?"

The analogy provided the VP with a new perspective on what it meant to work together, to win together. Approaching her counterpart, she focused on their points of commonality: they both wanted to be good leaders, for their teams to be seen as successful and to exceed expectations. Working together, these things were possible. The effect was immediate. Things that had been taking three months to accomplish before were now being wrapped up in weeks. Noticing the strain in the relationship, stepping towards each other and seeking ways to mitigate the tensions, provided this leader and those around her with new muscles for working together.

Perspective is a powerful skill. It lets you explore existing filters and examine the world through the lens of others, which is the secret to working together. *It's not about you!* How you act on new insights can make the difference between obstruction and resilience in your work with others.

From self-interest to the needs of the whole

A primary perspective shift in working together is from considering your own self-interest to thinking about the needs of the collective whole, from your needs to theirs.

It's all too easy to be seduced into thinking that getting the work done is the most important thing. You may believe that you put in what it takes to get the job done and that others

"You can change absolutely anything about your life when you first change the way you see it."

WAYNE DYER

should too. You harden—no one is patting your back, so why would you need to do so for others? Here we offer another outlook, which happens to be a true story.

Janelle was one busy person, with lots of new systems and processes to put into place, hundreds of people to rapidly onboard and integrate into systems, payroll to oversee, immigration compliance to manage. She was also a wife and mother. And too many nights, Janelle's boss would overhear her checking in with the family and remotely "tucking into bed" her two adorable kids. She was frequently at work, burning the midnight oil alongside her boss before facing the long trek back home.

As one major project was ending, Janelle's boss wanted to acknowledge her unwavering commitment and the sacrifices she had witnessed Janelle and her family making. The boss contemplated a spot bonus, but then decided on something more personal. She was aware that Janelle's husband was between jobs; Janelle was the sole bread winner for the family and extra niceties were not an option. And so she had it arranged for Janelle and her family to spend time at Disneyland, all expenses paid, including some pocket money for the kids. In the package presented to Janelle was a note, handwritten by her boss and addressed to Janelle's husband and kids, expressing a deep gratitude for sharing so much of their mom and wife with the company and acknowledging the many nights she was not at home.

Her boss's intention was to declare that Janelle was much more than a resource to the company and, as such, to offer meaningful acknowledgment for her efforts. It was to recognize her as a human with a full and wonderful life, one that the needs of the company were impacting. The boss also wanted to make sure the recognition was something that would create long-lasting memories for Janelle and her family.

It worked. After sharing lots of pictures from Disneyland, Janelle returned from her holiday and continued her loyal service to the company for many more years.

Co-Creating

One approach to creating deeper, more meaningful connections is "co-creating," an interactive way of working together. Co-creating is based on the belief that true collaboration allows much more creativity, brilliance and magic than doing something on your own. And that better ideas and solutions come when you don't force your perspective or will on others. Co-creating requires being supportive, letting go, being curious even in the face of challenges, not being attached to your own point of view, being open to any outcome and having faith in each other's power.

How do you co-create? Here are a few tips, tricks and techniques.

Quiet your internal know-it-all

Co-creating is about building something together. This dynamic process involves a lot of input from you and those you are working with. Sometimes you need to put aside what you think and stay curious about what *they* think. Your internal know-it-all is going to hate this. And yes, there are plenty of times when you need to add in your thoughts and wisdom. You know when to bring it, and if you don't know yet, you can always ask yourself, "Will what I have to offer move us forward?" or "What will serve us best right now?" If what you have to say is not part of the answer, resist. When you don't, you can inadvertently shut people down.

What can help quiet your internal know-it-all?

- Listen deeply and curiously at level 2 to tune in to what *the other person* knows.

- Get curious, genuinely curious, about the person or people who you are working with. What is their perspective? What might they see that you don't?

Practice, and see what you notice about creating more space for others.

Find others right

Finding other people right is a great skill that you can use at work and elsewhere to connect with other people, defuse difficult situations and arrive at better, more creative ideas. It's about listening deeply to another person so that they feel heard. This creates an environment of positivity and safety. People feel that their views are valued and welcome. A generative and collaborative atmosphere that is conducive to co-creation and meaningful connection results.

Finding other people right takes focus, commitment and creativity. The trick is to find something that the other has said right. That doesn't mean you have to find *everything* that they said right. This skill helps you listen more closely and builds trust, because you demonstrate your belief that there's value in the other person's perspective. It is a powerful way to demonstrate respect and collaboration.

You find something right about what another person said— and you build on it—even when they disagree with you or you disagree with them. For example, let's say the person you are co-creating with is Amos. You might say: "I want to underscore what Amos just said about [fill in the topic]. This is key because [add a meaningful aspect of Amos's perspective]."

Or if you have a thought that's not exactly the same as theirs, you find them right and then make a separate and distinct point. For example: "Amos brings up a really import-ant approach to [fill in the topic]. Another way of approaching the same thing is [say your point]."

Lastly, finding right can be a great way to build positive feelings in your work environment and emphasize a point that you think others may not have heard: "Amos just made a great point that I want to make sure we capture..."

This doesn't mean you agree with everything a person says, but you look for a little bit, at least 2 percent truth in their words. This is the opposite of defensiveness or making some-one else wrong when their point of view differs from yours. Surprisingly, if you look for it, you can always find at least 2 percent truth in what others say.

When you find others right, you create a safer, more open environment because it's okay to disagree. If you make others wrong, you shut down debate and dialogue, limiting creativity and collaboration. Finding right makes room for "and" instead of "or"... in other words, it allows that both ideas may have merit.

Let's be clear, this is not "going along to get along." Find-ing others right is a particularly helpful skill for those of you with a strong reactive tendency of control. Rather than assert-ing your control, you broaden your perspective to truly work with another human to bring something into being and to get things done.

Better Perspective, Part 2

Here are a few reflection points to start finding others right:

- What does *making people wrong* do?
- What gets in the way of finding others right?
- What gets created when you find the other person right?
- What would shift if you focused on ways to find others right?
- Where could you practice this skill?

_____

_____

_____

_____

_____

Mindset Shift: Outcome-Creating

This shift is about moving from problem-reacting to outcome-creating—to bring something you care about into being as opposed to reacting to the problem in front of you by trying to stop it and return to normal. Let's use an example of a classic messy moment in an organization: an edict drips down from upper management, and you must enact and champion it. You disagree with the direction and do not know what to do. It's your choice how you show up in those moments. Outcome-creating can help you find a new perspective and unlock a feeling of being stuck.

Late one afternoon, Debbie felt the presence of someone at her desk. It was Ang, a manager in the company who oversaw a pretty large team. Without looking up, Debbie could feel the agitation brewing within him. It turns out he had just left a meeting with two VPs of the company. They had informed him that his team would be splitting in two, with part of the team moving under one VP to support a new initiative and the rest of the team, including Ang, moving under the other VP.

He needed a safe place to vent about what was a happening. Ang disagreed with the decision from a business perspective. Breaking up the team was, in his opinion, the wrong approach. From where he stood, the decision makers didn't understand what his team did and how they worked as a unit to support both internal and external functions of the organization. There was tension in his relationship with the VP he would now report to and, according to Ang, they did not like each other. Ang did not trust the motives or the rationale behind the decision. He had worked hard to build his team and "they" were tearing it apart. In good faith he could not, would not, tell his team that this was a good change. He disagreed with all of it and was mad, hurt and lost.

That was a lot to unpack. Ang was caught between a rock and a hard place. He was powerless to stop this change and he disagreed with it. In the privacy of a breakout room, tears streamed down his cheeks as he talked about telling his team. He was hurting from a place of personal loss—he really valued his team and their work. He was firmly stuck in the perspective that this was not a good idea: for them, the business or himself. And he believed his team would look to him for reassurance that it was. This is one of those messy moments when staying in the hard times can help you grow. The challenge was for Ang to choose a perspective he could lead from with his integrity intact.

Step one was to acknowledge all the hurt, disappointment and shock that he was feeling. You can't rush it, and you can't

If you don't deal with internal tension and figure out what your role is in it, you just drag that baggage along with you.

skip over this part. For Ang, a shitty thing was happening. He had worked hard to create a high-functioning team and now he felt it was being disbanded. It was important for him to have his feelings around this.

Step two was some perspective work. The decision had been made. It was reality, and as much as Ang might not like it, it was going to happen. With Debbie's guidance, they explored Ang's perspective. First, he sat in the idea that the VPs were wrong and short-sighted, but then what? Another perspective was, what were the implications to the business if they did nothing? Yet another perspective to explore was whether they were right. What if this decision was in the best interests of the team and the organization? Ang tried on all of these viewpoints. He challenged himself in the safety of that room to find a new perspective—one that was not about him but about success for the team and the company.

Step three was to help him shift into this new perspective and combine it with the outcome he wanted to create: success for the organization and the team. What would be possible when this occurred? Debbie and Ang talked for a long time about what he could say to his team that was true and honest from this perspective. That is what the team needed from him, expected from him. They trusted him. And the company trusted him to lead his team. This was a both/and moment for Ang. After exploring different perspectives and choosing his own, he delivered what was needed by both the team and the organization. He let them know how much he treasured the team they had become. They were built to be resilient and to serve the best interests of the company. And they were being called on to do just that. The personal bonds and connections they had created would last beyond a reporting structure.

These types of organizational decisions are made all the time. What is important is how Ang asked for help and constructively sorted through the internal tension he experienced so he could help his team move forward with the speed and resilience the organization needed. Without compromising his values or his care for the team, Ang widened his lens, shifting his point of view away from the loss he felt to what might be in the best interests of the team and the organization. He held firmly on to the outcome he needed to create: to maintain a relationship with his team grounded in trust and honesty.

Sometimes the story does not end so well. Gallup reports that people don't leave their companies, they leave their managers.[11] That can be a reflection of different values and perspectives and the inability of two people to constructively work through them. If they aren't dealt with positively, differences will get in the way of a healthy working relationship.

When it is too hard and you cannot find your way, sometimes leaving is the best thing to do, to find a place where you can be more fully expressed. But here's the bad news: if you don't deal with that internal tension and figure out what your role is in the break-up, you just drag that baggage along with you and it will repeat itself. Work is hard; people are messy. And you are one of them. Deal with your stuff—don't put it on others. When relationships fail, take out the microscope, claim your role in the failure and figure out what you could have done differently.

Change happens all the time: strategy, direction, tactics, leaders, manager, teams. People evolve. Organizations evolve. You evolve. There will be opposing perspectives, and it can be uncomfortable. Perspective is about choosing how you want to look at a situation. It provides an opportunity to be generative with the outcome rather than reactive. You choose your perspective, including one that may be new and different, one that will broaden your understanding of the people around you and make working together better.

5

claiming
values

MOST PEOPLE ARE unconscious about their core beliefs and what really matters to them on a fundamental level. Claiming values helps you become conscious of what drives your behavior and articulate what is important to you and why. Knowing your values creates intentionality. It allows you to stand in choice about how you are being and what you spend your time and energy doing. It creates clarity in your life. It means you *know what is important to you.*

Imagine This

You are not the same person you were when you were twenty, thirty, forty or whatever age. You are changing all the time. And so are the things that you value. As you gain life experiences, what matters to you shifts and modifies. Perhaps you start out focused on your career or making money or traveling. Perhaps you have a child and that becomes your focus. Then a health scare alters your priorities. The dream boss you joined the company for leaves. You change and life changes. In the midst of this, ask yourself who you are becoming and what you want.

- What do you have and not have?
- What are you tolerating, and what do you need to let go of?
- What do you need to step into?

These are good questions to ask from time to time. They will help you to stay present to how you are evolving, and to claim values for yourself and connect that to what happens around you. Claiming values means knowing what is important to you and living from that. As Viola Davis says: "I believe that the privilege of a lifetime is being who you are, truly being who you are."[1]

Connecting Alignment and Productivity

Businesses are composed of individuals who collectively create productivity. It's important to align people on business objectives and outcomes, and businesses spend a ton of valuable time working towards this alignment. But they don't always account for the humans doing this work. They neglect to help people connect what they do to why they do it, for the company and for themselves. Yet when people feel connected to what they are doing, they are more productive and engaged.

Alignment and engagement are two sides of the same coin, and both are important. It's naive to think you can fully realize one without the other. Imaginasium (isn't that a cool company name?) researched these two concepts and offers up a terrific distinction:

- **Alignment:** This is "the head." It's the logical approach—setting the course, the vision and the brand promise. It's making sure the team members *understand* the goals, their roles, how all the pieces fit together, and what success means to them and the organization.

- **Engagement:** This is "the heart." It's emotional—it focuses on how people *feel* about where things are going. Do they agree? How do they feel about what's being asked of them, and do they care enough to give it their all? (More on this in chapter 7.)

Organizations spend an inordinate amount of time trying to wrap people's heads around where the business is going, but they fall short of engaging people's hearts. Imaginasium continues: "There are plenty of organizations out there with incredibly passionate and loyal employees. But if they're not aligned around a core purpose, achievable goals and role clarity, they're like a bunch of rowers in a boat each doing their own thing. They're likely to go somewhere, but not efficiently or without a great deal of confusion."[2]

Alignment is about defining the reality. As a leader, you must show folks where your vision will take them and what strategy will get them there. It's also important to connect what the organization is doing to why that matters to you. You show the way, and in doing so you open the door for your people to connect their own values to those of the organization. Aligning minds and engaging hearts: a winning combination.

When alignment is clear, you attract quality talent and retain the talent you already have. This is important for productivity. According to Gallup, organizations with the highest performers have three things going for them:

- They have tenures of a decade or more in their organizations.
- Employees are engaged in their work.
- People are in roles where the expectations of the job align well their innate talents.

Each variable affects outcomes on its own, but the highest performance comes from the combination of these three factors.[3]

You get to determine how you show up in the world moving forward. It starts with knowing what is important to you.

It's a plain and simple truth: Actively engaged and aligned employees drive organizations further, faster. And this improves productivity.

Unearthing your core values

Values guide the alignment of your thoughts, words and behaviors. Values are central to who you are; claiming them is core to who you aspire to be. Claiming your values starts with clarifying your purpose in life, what Simon Sinek refers to as your WHY,[4] and then becoming conscious of how you live that purpose day-to-day.

Values are so ingrained within you that you may be unaware of them, unable to give them voice. Jane Finette is the co-founder of be radical, a company focused on teaching, building and nurturing a community of radicals who see a different path, a different future, and are ready to make it happen. She shares: "I was in my early thirties and never had an opportunity to look at what had been holding me back, what I genuinely cared about. After participating in the leadership program offered by Debbie and Kate, I felt so out of sorts with what I was put on this planet to do. It was not marketing in my current organization anymore. While my values were deeply aligned with the organization, the work I did every day was not what I was called to do."

With this newfound awareness, Jane quit her job and established the Coaching Fellowship, a nonprofit organization that provides leadership development and pro bono executive coaching to extraordinary emerging women leaders. She has since co-founded be radical. Jane credits the work she did to discover her core values as the catalyst for developing personally as a leader and launching her leadership program. "It awakened parts of me that I was unaware of." She had known something wasn't "right" but never had the tools to figure it out. "It was exhilarating *and* terrifying!" recalls Jane.[5]

Values are a residual of your life's story, a by-product of your past. They are imprinted in you through your family, your culture and your communities. Your past has shaped who you are and it forms your identity. But here's a defining secret: although your past has shaped who you are so far, you get to choose how you are for the rest of your life. You get to determine how you show up in the world moving forward. And it starts with knowing what is important to you.

When Kate was younger and working in the advertising industry, she thought that some pretty poor behavior dominated the workplace: some sleeping around, people being pressured into work decisions, the kind of stuff that made her skin crawl a bit (or a lot). There were things that just did not sit "right" with her sensibilities, but she could not put her finger on why.

At one point, two of her bosses decided to hide the truth about a particular matter from a client. They did not want to come clean, and this did not feel right to Kate. When the client asked her outright about the issue, Kate knew she had a choice: tell the truth and risk being fired or lie to the client. She decided to tell the truth, knowing that she was jeopardizing her job. She also decided, if this was how the organization wanted to be, then she did not want to be a part of the organization.

Kate was not fired and to this day she is not sure whether anyone else knew about what she shared with the client. However, she does remember becoming aware about how important it is for her to be able to live with herself—to have a clear conscience about how she is with others. That became a beacon for her, a guide for decision making. Kate had revealed one of her core values: integrity.

Like younger Kate, most of you will need to do some unearthing of your core values. Once you have discovered them, you then get to determine how you will live them. You are worthy of living a life true to who you are and how you want to be in this world. You get to choose.

How Claiming Values Produces Alignment

Alignment is about living your values and having continuity and consistency between what you say and what you do. Alignment also creates clarity at work. Almost every organization will have a list of values they claim as important. Most values statements inform customers and employees about the organization's top priorities and core beliefs. Forty, a user-experience design group, conducted research on the values statements of hundreds of companies.[6] They identified an unsurprising list of commonalities:

Accountability	Openness
Collaboration	Passion
Commitment	People
Community	Quality
Customer focus	Respect
Diversity	Responsibility
Excellence	Safety
Honesty	Service
Innovation	Teamwork
Integrity	Trust

Nothing is particularly impressive or remarkable about this list. Nothing too disruptive or controversial. These seem like important qualities of being a good company to work for. Although these words show up in employee handbooks and on plaques around the office, organizations often fail to turn these thoughtful words into meaningful behaviors. Your organization may value respect, but respect means different things to people based on their life stories and backgrounds.

These words are often elusive and undefined, in part because how we work together is not given the same value as what work gets done. The activity of people gets rewarded: making the numbers, meeting the goal, delivering the product. Too often the behaviors that create a positive work environment go uncelebrated. Behaviors are values in action, and they matter to people. In the void between words and meaning, how people feel about work gets lost. When someone finally notices the disconnect, usually because of turnover or underperformance, it is often too late.

Our client Clever Inc. is one of the best examples we have experienced of bringing core values to life in an organization. Founded in 2012, Clever is a widely used single sign-on platform for K–12 education. Our work with Clever was to help their leadership build credibility and trust, which in turn would empower people to make the whole organization better. Tyler Bosmeny, Clever's co-founder and CEO, shares, "We approached company culture with intention right from the start because we believed that making Clever a great place to work would help us do great work. When Clever was just getting started, I remember meeting with Alfred Lin, former COO of Zappos, who encouraged us to start thinking intentionally about our culture. As a team, we created a set of values to shape our behaviors, approach, and workspace—the Clever Culture Tenets." In short, these are:

- Leave the classroom better than you found it.
- Do the extra credit. (In other words, go above and beyond to make projects great.)
- Clever is a group project.
- Don't trust the textbook. (Question how things are done.)

- Always be a student.
- Bring good vibes.[7]

The Clever Culture Tenets are the responsibility of the Clever community, and they are embedded in every way the company operates. The company reinforces the tenets through rituals and celebration. One example of this is Culture Kudos. Every week, Clever team members recognize one another for demonstrations of the Culture Tenets. In addition to a small donation to a charity of their choice, recipients receive the coveted Clever collector's coin, featuring the tenet they are being recognized for. Clever's intentional and collaborative culture was acknowledged as an *Inc.* 2019 Best Workplace. Kudos to the Clever community for showing the way to make humanity work better!

An organization—be it a company, school, church, motorcycle club, retirement village or any other group—is a community. And that community is a reflection of its people. You, and all others who are part of a shared community, are living, breathing representations of its values. Your collective behaviors reflect what is important to you. As renowned leadership authority, educator and organizational consultant Stephen Covey said, "Personal leadership is the process of keeping your vision and values before you and aligning your life to be congruent with them."[8]

Core Skill: Acknowledgment

It sounds straightforward to align your life so there is congruence between what you are doing and how you are being. However, too often people are unaware of why something matters deeply to them. And even when they are, people spend a great deal of energy trying to hide qualities they think don't belong in the workplace. It can be difficult to acknowledge who you are, to claim the character of your being. We rarely dig deep into our values, and certainly not in the workplace. Acknowledgment is a skill that gives voice to qualities that you see in yourself or in another person. Hearing the characteristics that others see in you can help you claim the values that are important to you. You can create meaningful change in your workplace, and we offer acknowledgment as a way to find resonance within yourself and with others.

Most of us long to be seen, really, truly, deeply seen by another human being, for the person we are and the person we aspire to be. Being seen touches and opens your heart. When Mary Colvig participated in leadership training with Debbie and Kate, she experienced an awakening during one exercise. Mary had always felt good about her skills and ability to build relationships with others. But in the high-tech environment she was working in, she felt they were frowned upon: "I felt pressure to assimilate and adjust to the very engineering-driven culture that was aggressive, loud and outspokenly critical. It was hard to be heard and feel respected in the organization."

During the training, Mary was encouraged to be her unfiltered self, and she was acknowledged by her peers for her "superhero strengths" as a relationship builder. She felt seen. The experience showed her that she had created her own limiting belief about the value of her relationship-building superpowers and revealed to her that she wasn't alone. When her colleagues were given the chance to acknowledge her as her most compelling self, Mary realized that they valued her soft skills. The attributes she had been constantly trying to quash to assimilate into the culture are now qualities she embraces wholeheartedly. She recalls this memory of "being seen" every day.

Learning to acknowledge another person is a message straight from your heart.

Better Acknowledgment

There are two simple steps to acknowledging:

- Deliver a short phrase that acknowledges the quality of who the person is or how they did something. For example, "You are so forthright and courageous in dealing with difficult questions" or "Your positive attitude when revising the work is infectious."

- Pause, and watch your message be received. You are witnessing another person learning about themselves.

_____

_____

_____

_____

_____

_____

_____

_____

_____

Notice the simplicity of these two steps. There is no preamble, no stage setting—based on our observations while teaching this skill to others, this is the hardest part. Learning to acknowledge another person is a message straight from your heart.

This acknowledgment was a catalyst for Mary. It allowed her to embrace who she is at her most compelling self, and the work got a lot better for her and her team. "I was able to get resources for my team. We got big things done with them. We built better relationships; everyone thrived."[9]

Acknowledgment has powerful application in all our practices, as it sends a message to others that particular characteristics of their being are seen and appreciated. It is powerful affirmation to be seen by another human being. It is a simple yet powerful skill that you can use liberally with others.

The skill of acknowledgment is when you recognize not just what the person has done, but the spirit of how they did it. You are looking to acknowledge a quality of who this person is.

How to claim your values

As the eldest child in a high-achieving family, Leland Franklin, founder and CEO of Kenshō Learning, grew up chasing all of the traditional measures of success—his entire life was focused on going to a good school, getting a high-paying job, and pursuing promotion after promotion to make his family proud. He developed a strong work ethic, grit and a dynamic skill set that helped him navigate the corporate world as a high achiever. Eventually, he landed a job that looked great on paper—leading a high-performing technical team at an education technology start-up. However, in reality, he was consistently in burnout, working eighty-plus hours a week on work that wasn't engaging, and he often felt empty inside.

Leland shares, "I would ask myself, 'Is this it?' I could feel in my heart that there had to be more. My work had become so abstract—leading a team of customer-facing engineers who provided consulting services to engineers at other companies—that I felt increasingly disconnected from the people I was originally trying to serve: students and teachers. As we grew, I made changes to my day-to-day responsibilities and worked on shifting my perspective on things, but the core feeling of emptiness persisted."

After navigating this dissatisfaction for almost two years, Leland decided enough was enough and took a leap of faith. He left his job to "explore"—which he considered a high risk in today's fast-paced world and a change that many of his peers were not comfortable with. "How can you leave your job without having something else lined up?" they asked. "You become so much less marketable to companies if you're not currently working... You're going to spend months unemployed."

In coming to the decision, Leland says, "I faced new levels of anxiety that I had never before imagined. I danced endlessly with internal voices of doubt and fear. Yet once I finally made the commitment within myself to make the leap, I felt a sense of deep peace wash over me." Leland notes the Rumi saying, "What you seek is seeking you." While he was saying yes to the most uncertainty he'd ever had in his professional life and going against all of the "shoulds," he felt grounded by a deep inner confidence that whispered, "You're on the right path. Keep going."

Declining interviews, he created the space and time for deep introspection, giving himself permission to inquire:

- "Throughout all of my different careers so far, what aspects have made me feel the most alive?"

- "In what situations have I felt like my unique gifts were best expressed?"

- "What is really important to me?"

- "What is the impact I want to make in this world?"

In that space, themes emerged. "I love helping other people believe in themselves, discover themselves, become more and create more. I am especially drawn to visionary, compassionate leaders who wish to spend their lives in service of something greater." A mentor encouraged him to enroll in an integral leadership coaching training program, and the very first class set something in him on fire. From that point on, people showed up in his life who provided opportunities for growth, learning and deep service. He opened his full-time practice as an executive coach for socially conscious leaders, and says, "The magic keeps on happening. My heart is full, my business is thriving, and I'm learning to live in this paradox of embracing the vast unknown, while knowing deep inside that I'm on the right path—my path."[10]

What is important to you? Underlying this question are your values. When you live by your values and bring them alive, your life will feel more fulfilling. We promise.

Some of your values you are already living. Some values you will find when they have been stepped on and you react. Don't be afraid to look there too. Identifying what is important to you and why is a crucial first step in the process. These insights let you spend the rest of your life developing your values so that you become the fullest expression of who you want to be. Your values might evolve over time, or they might alter as your life stage changes. When you acknowledge and name your values, it becomes much easier to live by them.

Your personal core values are there to guide your day-to-day behavior and choices; they are a compass to help you stay on track. They provide a way to navigate the decisions you face each day. In fact, you are always claiming values. This process is just about becoming aware of the values that motivate you. Once you give voice to your values, they can haunt you, taunt you, and can make you feel guilty for not living up to them. When you honor your values, you will live a more fulfilling life. Time to pay attention!

Better Alignment

First, answer this question: In my life right now, what is important to me?

Next, ask yourself at least five times: What is important about that?

Here's an example:

- **In my life right now, what is important to me?** "I want to travel to every part of the world."

- **What is important about that?** "There is so much to see and experience."

- **What is important about that?** "The more I experience, the more I learn about others."

- **What is important about that?** "I get new perspectives that help me question things I think and believe."

- **What is important about that?** "I want to be open to new ways of thinking and challenge my beliefs."

- **What is important about that?** "Maybe what I think is wrong."

- **What is important about that?** "It might cause me to act towards people in ways that are hurtful or disrespectful."

- **What is important about that?** "It's important to me that all people are respected."

- **What is important about that?** "Every human has value."

As you dig deeper, you will find emotion (that is your heart talking to you). You will feel your answers rather than think about the "right" thing to say. Speak them out loud and notice when your voice shifts from thinking to feeling. This is resonance. You will feel it. The deeper you go, the closer you will get to your core values. Don't give up. Stay with it when it gets hard, when the answers don't come quickly and when it is uncomfortable. You are worth it!

_____

_____

_____

_____

_____

_____

_____

_____

_____

_____

_____

_____

_____

_____

_____

_____

_____

_____

The shift here is to go from thinking you have no control to knowing what is important to you. You train the people around you how to treat you. The more conscious you are about how you want to be in this world, the more you can create that for yourself. This is important—your life matters.

Mindset Shift: Navigating Resistance

Navigating resistance and claiming values is about staying in relationship with others when it is hard, when it is tough, and when doing what needs to be done is not what you want to do or not what others want done. The shift here is to step towards the resistance to find where your values align with what needs to be done—and act from there.

Some of the best moments to grow as a leader come during those hard, challenging times. Debbie was working with a company that had an underperforming business unit. The CEO had to close down the unit and redeploy most of its people onto existing projects, and he was struggling. The sales team for the business unit would lose their jobs. It was the first time in the company's history that they were facing role elimination. Every member of this tight-knit community was valued. Despite the unsuccessful nature of this specific business venture, the folks working in the unit had poured their hearts into it. It was just bad market timing.

These are truly the hardest decisions we see CEOs have to make. The weight of these types of decisions is monumental and, in our experience, they are not made lightly. Debbie met with the CEO to support his communications efforts, and it became clear that not only had he never eliminated jobs in this company, but he'd also never cut jobs anywhere. After acknowledging that he had made the toughest decision

Step towards resistance

to find where your values
align with what needs to be
done—and act from there.

possible but one that was necessary for the longer-term health of the company, Debbie focused in on what his communications would be to the impacted team and to the rest of the company's workforce.

He truly wanted to stay in alignment with his own values as well as the values of the company. It was impressive to work with and witness a leader so committed to these values. Debbie worked with him to articulate the big risk the company took with this venture; how visible the effort had been and how hard it became. They talked about the decision-making process he used and what he noticed in that. They talked about fear and how actions like eliminating jobs can scare and confuse people. And they talked about what the company needed to hear from him.

It was one of the most honest, heartfelt and straightforward messages we have seen a CEO deliver. The DNA of the company was about taking risks, he said, and sometimes that will mean failure. Not because folks didn't try but because sometimes you are ahead of the market with your ideas. He noted that as CEO he has to hold the short- and long-term needs of the company. The potential reward was too elusive, given the investments of people, attention and money. He shared that this was one of the hardest decisions he had made and openly talked about the weight of the decision, knowing people of their community would be impacted. He reassured the company that those they had said goodbye to were treated well, and again acknowledged being grateful for their valiant efforts on the company's behalf. He closed by challenging those in the room to keep taking risks, to keep pushing, to keep on learning. He reassured them that, as a company, they would take more risks. And they would fail again, because failure is part of how they learn and grow. The CEO's compassion was felt by those affected by the layoffs, who knew that this was not something that the CEO wanted. And his transparency created alignment within the organization.

When you align what needs to be done with your own values, your leadership is compelling. Be aware of what is important to you. Consciously choose to live your life aligned with your values and have the courage to stand in them during the tough, messy moments.

6

owning
your
impact

O WNING YOUR IMPACT drives accountability because it creates more integrity between what you do and how you do it. Your impact is how people experience you. When you take responsibility for your impact, it creates personal accountability; your words and your actions align. You deliver what is needed to drive results and you do it in manner consistent with your character. Owning your impact is a practice of *being responsible for what you create.*

Imagine This

In 2013, Lululemon CEO Chip Wilson had an impact moment. In an interview with a reporter, he indicated that complaints about the quality of Lululemon's expensive yoga pants were unfounded, and implied that the problem was the size of the women wearing them—that their thighs were too large. Oops. Wilson said on Bloomberg TV, "Quite frankly, some women's bodies just don't work for it [the yoga pants]."

The reporter clarified, "So, more likely that they will be see-through on some women's bodies than others?"

"No, I don't think that way," Wilson replied. "Even our small size would fit an extra-large. You know, it's really about the rubbing through the thighs, how much pressure is there, over a period of time and how much they use it."

Yet his impact didn't stop there. In Wilson's video apology, published on Facebook and YouTube, he said "I'm sad, I'm really sad. I'm sad for the repercussions of my actions. I'm sad for the people of Lululemon who I care so much about, that have really had to face the brunt of my actions." Yet, his customers felt he didn't apologize to the women he body-shamed. He simply apologized for the repercussions of his comments. People are not stupid; they know the difference. Soon after, Lululemon stocks fell nearly 4 percent and Wilson resigned from his role as Lululemon's chairman.[1]

Did Wilson realize the impact he was going to have when uttering those fateful words? Not necessarily, says Heidi Grant Halvorson in her book *No One Understands You and What to Do About It*. She writes, "I'm going to go out on a limb and suggest that Chip Wilson did not intend, with those poorly chosen words, to insult and alienate his loyal customer base... So, if that wasn't his intention, and if he's not an idiot (self-made billionaire, people), then what happened?"

Halvorson argues that "human beings have a surprisingly difficult time when it comes to knowing what exactly they are communicating" and that we often don't come across the way we intend. Yet, we can't figure this out on our own—we need to understand how other people see us to truly know our impact.[2]

We agree wholeheartedly. In our experience with leaders and teams, we've come to see that life is not just about what you do but who you are while you do it. The definition of impact is having an effect or influence. This is what we are talking about here. We are all impacting others, all the time. Yes, you. Don't buy into the narrative that you are not important or influential. Everyone matters; anyone who thinks they don't matter is wrong. Impact is something that, as we grow as humans, we need to pay attention to. It's important to look at, claim and understand your impact, intended or unintended. You are responsible for your impact.

Connecting Accountability and Productivity

When asked about their biggest challenge at work, CEOs most frequently responded, "accountability in the workplace."[3] A *Harvard Business Review* study backs this up, showing that almost 50 percent of managers fail to hold their people accountable.[4] Accountability leads to higher productivity and performance. What we mean by accountability is owning your impact and taking responsibility for doing what you say you will. It is both/and, not either/or. Imagine how different the story above would have gone if Chip Wilson had taken responsibly for the mess he created, apologized for his error in judgment and the impact it had on others and then identified how Lululemon was fixing the problem!

As a leader, you are accountable to yourself and for the impact you have on the people around you. You influence how people feel about the work they are producing. In his article "Why Accountability Matters in the Workplace," Sean Pomeroy points out that "the American Psychological Association's 2018 Work and Well-Being Survey found that 91% of employees who feel valued at their job are motivated to do their best, compared with 41% of those who don't feel valued. It's a domino effect: Low accountability leads to mistrust, which leads to low morale, which leads to worker devaluation, which leads to low engagement, which leads to low productivity."[5]

Accountability has big reverberations inside an organization's culture. It can create safety for people to fully contribute in a shame-free zone where great work can co-exist alongside errors or mistakes. We are all humans. As a leader you show the way by taking responsibility for your actions and the impact they create on others.

Discovering Your Impact

A funny, maybe not-so-funny, story happened one day when Debbie was the chief people officer of a high-tech company. Her executive assistant gave her feedback that people on the team thought she was in a bad mood. When Debbie asked, "What's that all about?" the EA commented that she'd failed to say "good morning" to folks on her way into the office. When she had walked in that morning, Debbie had just finished a distracting phone call. She had created an unintended impact on those around her. The team knew she cared about them, but on that morning, she was unavailable to them. In the absence of context, people began to make up stuff about Debbie and how she was feeling towards them.

Believe it or not, you are influencing others *all* the time. Yep, it's true. You create an impact when you walk into a room. If you have positional power—if you're a leader, a manager, someone who makes decisions for all or part of your organization—people are paying particular attention to your behavior.

Sometimes your impact is intended, and sometimes it is not. When it is intended, you create the effect you mean to. Unintended? Like Debbie in the story above, you have no idea of your influence on people or a situation. We love the word "unintended," because it's so human. An unintended impact is just that: accidental, unplanned, inadvertent. It takes some conscious awareness for you to notice your impact. To be aware of it, you have to listen at level 2 (to the other) or level 3 (to the environment).

Kate coaches a man at a tech company. He has reached a level of expertise in his field at a very early stage in his career. He has no direct reports but rather works across the company as needed. He has a deep understanding of the product technology of the organization. So, in one way, he has no direct positional power, and yet in another, his technical expertise is so vast that he garners tremendous respect within the company.

The work that he and Kate have been doing together is to help him claim the impact he wants to have on the company: on the technical product (of course), but also beyond that, on the culture of the organization—how he wants to be known and where the company is headed. Much of the work that they have done has been on his realizing, to begin with, that he does have an impact. Then, the second part is for him to become more conscious of the impact he wants to have.

To create this awareness, Kate coached him to ask himself these questions:

- "What impact am I having?"
- "Is that the impact that I want to have?"
- "If not, what is the impact that I want to have?"

In the work that many of us do, we are oblivious not only of our faults but often even more of our strengths. We take for granted those things that we do really, really well—our Olympic strengths—and so one of our jobs is to continue to stay aware of what those are too. When you give yourself permission to move beyond what you think is expected of you and free yourself to be who you are, it feels like taking flight. There is a liberation, a freedom and a relaxing into who you get to be. You stop pretending, stop trying so hard. You can just be who you are.

Kate remembers the moment when she could finally relax and see that the impact she has is enough. In fact, it is more than enough! She is compelling when she creates a sense of warmth, fun and play and makes people laugh. She realized her impact as a leader is straightforward; it is about being who she genuinely is and taking responsibility for the impact that can have on her relationships with others. Just being and knowing that it is enough is a *huge* relief.

Where do you begin to learn about owning your impact? It is, in fact, by seeking insights outside yourself.

You cannot figure out your impact on your own. The very nature of what we mean by impact is that you need other people to help you see what it is. One great technique to understand your impact is a good 360, which is an assessment that gathers input from your key stakeholders. While there are many 360 tools on the market, the one we prefer is the Leadership Circle Profile for useful, actionable insights about your impact on others.

Another technique is to ask people around you for specific insights into how you are being and how that affects them. For example, it's all too easy for leaders to focus single-pointedly on project status. Running the table during a full-team meeting and asking a direct report "Where are we at on project X?" can easily throw folks into the back of their chair and put them on the defensive. Probably not the impact you intend. You can pick up some of this reaction by watching their behaviors with level 3 listening or asking for direct feedback from the folks on your team. But don't seek feedback about what you are doing (for example, driving results); be curious about how you are being (forceful and direct) and how that's affecting people (maybe intimidating and threatening).

If you want to be seen or known as approachable, this style of running the table may not be creating the impact you want. You might try leading the meeting in a different way. Start by giving the team context for what you are listening for: "I'm curious where we all are on our projects because I am trying to navigate what I am seeing in the pipeline." Letting them in, in this way, might shift your impact to be more approachable.

What makes you compelling?

Do you know what makes you compelling? Do any of us know, really? Here, we define "compelling" as having a powerful and irresistible effect, eliciting acute admiration, attention and/or respect. When you are being compelling, people want to be around you; you have a quality of attraction. The funny thing is you simply cannot figure it out on your own. To see yourself in this way, you need the reflection from others. You need to begin to look outside of yourself.

Pascal Finette, co-founder of be radical (you met his wife, Jane, earlier), went through an exercise with us. This exercise asks for others to help you see how you show up in your organization, by assigning you particular characteristics. It shows you who you are at your most compelling. Pascal found it to be "deeply transformative—it feels very weird, joyful and funny, but it is meant to push you beyond your filter and let your real self show up. The goal is to be truly seen by others." Pascal reflects, "As a leader, we spend time on self-reflection, but we don't reflect too much on how we are seen by others, by our peers." Pascal notes that knowing how others see him and owning the impact of this affects him to this day, that he can keep showing up as his real, compelling self.[6]

All too often, you work hard to present a side of yourself to the world that you believe the world wants to see from you. This tendency is especially strong in the workplace environment. For example, people often attempt to present qualities of "determination" and "competence." They sacrifice the expression of other compelling, sometimes more quirky or intriguing aspects of themselves for the sake of wanting to appear competent and determined at all costs. Entire work cultures often form around an unconsciously chosen commitment to the expression of these qualities. The organizational expression of determination and competence can be reflected in a dour, serious, stress-filled atmosphere. They mean business, and that means they have to take it very seriously! Yet you are stifled and not fully expressed. You may get your job done, but you pay a huge price by denying the expression of your authentic self.

"Looking good" can prevent you from noticing what makes you compelling. You want to look good, be smart, the smartest in the room, at anyone's expense. A lot of organizations reward this behavior. But looking good can also be a trap. It can rob you of the authenticity that comes with feeling comfortable "in your own skin."

Unlocking your authenticity and that of your co-workers is a powerful way to bring more humanity into the workplace. From their study of twenty-one best companies to work for, Michael O'Malley and Bill Baker conclude, "Given our findings, it is safe to say that, today, too many businesses function with only their own interests in mind. If the presumption is that capable, profit-making management should put money before people, then our vision is terribly flawed. These flaws are due not necessarily to a failed exegesis of how markets work, but to gross misconceptions of how people work. The organizations we studied have given themselves the best chance to succeed by recognizing the human as the heart of the workplace, the thing that keeps everything else running."[7]

When you are authentic and genuinely being yourself, you are more compelling to others. Most people have a stronger desire to connect and work with people who are in alignment with their true, compelling self. HumanityWorks is devoted to helping people in organizations liberate themselves from this place of "looking a certain way" to being their joyful, heartfelt, goofy, funny, weird, wonderful, compelling selves.

Being compelling starts with **letting go of trying to be someone you are not.**

Better Impact

Being compelling starts with letting go of trying to be someone you are not. Begin by expanding your awareness: How you are showing up for others, and what impact do you create? Some places to get curious:

- **Do you make people laugh? How does that shift the room?** Possible answers: "The impact lightens the mood or problem" or "it causes hurtful injury to another."

- **Do you simply tell the truth with no drama?** Possible answers: "This helps calm the situation" or "this shuts people down."

- **Do you create a warm and inviting environment?** Possible answers: "This creates connection" or "this causes confusion."

- **Do you create stillness and a sense of reverence?** Possible answers: "This makes people feel safe" or "people feel scared."

- **Do you create clarity?** Possible answers: "This paves the way for straightforward decision making" or "it closes the door on the ideas of others."

- **Do you create a sense that anything is possible?** Possible answers: "This creates opportunity" or "it causes chaos."

- **Do you go deep on topics?** Possible answers: "Others experience a sense of discovery" or "they aren't able to follow along."

What impact do you create?

_____

_____

_____

_____

_____

_____

Linking Impact and Accountability

Your compelling self creates an impact. You have to seek feedback to know if your efforts are being received in the way that you intend. And if not, take responsibility for that impact. This creates personal accountability—your words and your actions are aligned. You continue to drive results and you do it in a manner that is consistent with your character.

The truth is, you are influencing all the time. Some of your impact is intended, and some not. In most organizations, leaders are so focused on delivering results that they don't take responsibility for how they deliver them. People do not tend to take responsibility for their behavior, particularly when it is "bad."

When you begin to take responsibility, you will create stronger accountability in all relationships throughout your organizations and your life. If you are willing to take responsibility for your impact, it strengthens your accountability with others. The accountability has more meaning because it is more authentic.

Back to O'Malley and Baker. In O'Malley's article about their work, he writes about the Motley Fool, a private investment firm that has adopted "foolishness" as a company value based on the fool in the Shakespeare play *As You Like It*. Fools have permission to speak truthfully and honestly about what they see, because they are not bound by the same constraints as the rest of the community. The fool can say things to the king that others cannot. Combined with the value of honesty, the Motley Fool creates a work environment in which people feel comfortable expressing themselves not just physically, but verbally as well. O'Malley and Baker concluded that "the ability to be authentic at your job is life-affirming: an outward expression of who we are and what we stand for. In this regard, authenticity also has a nonobvious effect. People who behave in accord with their values have stickier work ethics. They are more morally engaged, less deferent to circumstance, and will choose principle over the enticement."[8]

Charge EPC has a people-first culture with a foundational focus on empowering and supporting their employees. They are a leading provider of design, procurement and construction services for the West Coast utility industry. Billy Kilmer is the founder and COO. Billy has been in construction his entire life and he's used to getting big things done, being the one in charge, the one who knows how to move the ball down the road.

A wake-up call came for Billy when he realized he was not having the impact he wanted with the people around him and, in particular, with his business partner, Mike Robirds. Billy had a habit of playing cat-and-mouse when problems arose. Something would happen because of something Billy did or did not do, and he would wait for Mike to get mad. Then Billy would feel guilty, jump in to fix the problem and go back to the same behaviors that had caused the problem in the first place. "The impact I had on people wasn't always what I wanted or expected to have. And when I sensed this, I would ask for forgiveness, but then not change. I'd do it all over again." He realized this behavior was damaging his relationship with Mike and he needed to take ownership for it and change. His behavior was impacting the health of their partnership and, by extension, the company. Billy knew a big shift was needed.

Billy and Mike began tandem coaching with Debbie and Kate. In this format they each received feedback through 360s and individual coaching. Once a month we all came together to work through roadblocks and better ways of working together. Billy notes, when coaching with Kate, "she made me look in the mirror and ask, '*Why* do I keep doing this?'" He realized the guilt game wasn't working for him, and he began to take ownership of it.

Billy and Mike have created shared agreements that keep them aligned, one of which is "no surprises." Billy no longer goes into business meetings wondering what will come up and how he and Mike will react. They show up as a unit, having agreed in advance upon their position and goals. Their team has noticed the difference.

"Construction is cutthroat! You have to fight to keep it," Billy shares. "As a construction company we've always had physical safety in mind, but psychological safety wasn't on my radar. Our work with Kate and Debbie has given me insight into this type of safety. Learning about how my actions and words can impact others caused a big shift in the way I work with them." He calls the results "eye-awakening. You don't know what you don't know until you've gone through this process." Billy adds, "Our work with Kate and Debbie has helped me realize that for our company to be truly successful, the employees needed to drive this success, not me. Instead of solving the problems, I need to coach them on how to do that, on how to lead themselves to make the place better, and, in fact, make the world better."[9]

You are responsible for your impact

In knowing about yourself, you can begin to take responsibility for the impact you create. The first step is to become aware of your own impact. The next is to take responsibility for it. Think about this: What was your intended impact—the thing that you meant to have happen? Maybe it was to make someone feel good about something that they did well, or maybe to challenge them. Then think about the unintended impact—the thing you did not mean to have happen. It could be a joke that did not land as you intended, or maybe a sarcastic comment that offended someone.

The truth is that you cannot control the unintended or even intended impacts. Life will get messy, and at times you will land in a way that you did not intend. You cannot and will not be perfect at owning your impact. But you can begin to become aware of it. And if something has landed unintentionally, then you can take responsibility for it.

What does taking responsibility for your impact look like? Well, how much time do you have? It can look about a million different ways! It depends on the situation, what impact you had or didn't have, who it was with and any consequences that arose out of it. Usually, understanding your impact will take the form of a conversation. Curiosity and listening skills will really help you out here. If you want to grow, then stay curious and find out more. Listen to what others are telling you about yourself and ask, "Is that how I want to be perceived?" That is taking responsibility for your impact. Not defending or getting defensive, not arguing or getting high and mighty about it. Not that, please, not that. If you stay in the conversation, you might learn something about yourself. And if you show up with genuine curiosity, you have a much better chance of learning something new. This is being responsible for what you create.

What can happen for some people is that they begin to notice a quality about themselves, "Hey, I tell it like it is. I am a truth teller." And that is it! This narrative becomes carte blanche for them to spout their truth as though it is *the* truth. You might be a truth teller, and it can be easy to get a little high on telling your truth, when in fact, it is just *your* truth not *the* truth. Your perspectives influence what you hear and see and respond to. That creates an impact on others that is not in your control. Thus, you need to do a two-step to not only be aware of your impact but also take responsibility for it.

Recently, Kate was coaching a brilliant woman who is the head of analytics at a successful tech company. This client, Emily, said something that literally took Kate's breath away. Emily had received some feedback from the senior folks at her organization. They said something along the lines of, "You are always so thoughtful in how you respond to problems we are struggling with. You really think things through. And we want you to talk more in our director-level meetings." Emily said to Kate, "So, they like that I don't rush to judgment. That I take my time and provide a thoughtful response, yet they want me to speak without thinking." And Kate thought, "My gosh, it's so true: the very thing they love about Emily is what they want her to change!" This conversation between Kate and Emily quickly turned to impact. Was Emily having the impact that she wanted and that the company needed?

In many organizations, often the loudest (or the most senior) voice in the room gets heard. It therefore stands to reason that you may not be hearing from everyone, which means you are missing some important information from introverted and less dominant voices. By no means did Kate or Emily think that she should begin to do what they were asking. That would diminish her most compelling qualities. But they did brainstorm ways that she could have more immediate impact.

- She could ask for what she needs. She might say something like, "I would be happy to provide you with my thoughts on that and would like some time to think about this. I can get that to you in 24/48 hours. Will that work for you?"

- She could buddy up with someone in the room. She might find someone who can help her "get the floor." That person might say, "Hang on a minute. Emily has something to say." Then Emily could take the floor.

- She could let people in. Things move fast. Even if she didn't have an answer, introverted Emily could let people know she was thinking about something! She could offer up a question, something like, "So, one of the questions I am wondering about is..." Posing a question can be just as powerful as offering a solution. And sometimes even more so.

This feedback caused Kate and Emily to explore the kind of impact that she wanted to have but wasn't achieving. This is a big topic for both introverts and extroverts. Susan Cain's book *Quiet* is one we cannot recommend highly enough. Cain writes:

> If we assume that quiet and loud people have roughly the same number of good (and bad) ideas, then we should worry if the louder and more forceful people always carry the day. This would mean that an awful lot of bad ideas prevail while good ones get squashed. Yet studies in group dynamics suggest that this is exactly what happens. We perceive talkers as smarter than quiet types—even though grade-point averages and SAT and intelligence test scores reveal this perception to be inaccurate.[10]

Cain is also writing about impact here. Doesn't this extend to the idea that extroverts are having a bigger impact than introverts?

When you get a piece of feedback like Emily did, it is an opportunity to go digging. It does not mean you have to do that thing. It may be an opportunity to consider: Are you having the impact that you want? Do you need to take responsibility for something that happened? It can be time to explore and try a few things. It is an opportunity to take responsibility for what you created. By doing that, you create real accountability.

Core Skill: Shared Agreements

The skill of shared agreements can help you own your impact and drive accountability between yourself and others. Too often, relationships—at work and in life—start without time spent clarifying what each party needs to make the relationship work. Shared agreements create a pause so you can discuss and agree to what each person needs in order to work well together. Accountability is created by honoring those agreements, and if you mess up, they provide a safe way to take responsibility for any unintended impact.

It is all too common to jump into the doing of work without clarifying how you will work together. Here's an example: You're working with Jody on a project, and suddenly, Jody is updating your boss on your progress. You get in a huff because Jody should know she's not supposed to update your boss. You're supposed to do that! And Jody should know that is your responsibility. Jody, however, is oblivious that anything is wrong or that you are really mad. In the meantime, you are over in the corner pissed off at Jody and may have vented your irritation with a few other willing ears. Boom! Conflict is born.

"You never know when
a moment and a few
sincere words can have
an impact on a life."

ZIG ZIGLAR

But you now need to ask yourself: Have you clarified your expectations with Jody? Have you talked about how the two of you will work together on the project and how updates will be done? Have you talked about how you will work together if a line has been crossed or feelings are hurt? The clear answer in this situation with Jody is no. These are hidden assumptions that need to be unearthed. Shared agreements will solve this type of conflict and grease the wheels for more accountability and a more productive partnership.

The objective of shared agreements is simple: you want to clarify working relationships, with each person taking responsibility for their contribution to the relationship and to collectively agreed-upon outcomes. It helps unearth assumptions for how you will work together. Those assumptions are there; often you just aren't aware of them! (We joke that most conflicts can be traced back to whether your shared agreements were effective or not.)

Shared agreements are a living, breathing conversation and negotiation. Just because the other person has asked for something does not mean that you have to give it. Pay attention to what you are willing to do and what you are not willing to do. If you are not willing to do that thing, then make a counteroffer. For example, "I am not willing to take the notes all the time, but I will share that responsibility with you."

Here is another tip: you don't have to call it a shared agreement. Trust us... we work with a lot of engineers who would roll their eyes at us if we talked about "shared agreements." Make the idea approachable to your audience. You can just say, "Hey, let's talk about how we are going to work together. What do you need? Here's what I need." You will likely have to lead the conversation, because this is a new concept for most people.

At HumanityWorks we use this skill in all areas of our life. When Kate and her husband, George, and his two daughters, Catherine and Anna, moved into her house, they sat down and talked about shared agreements. Catherine was twenty at the time and Anna was seventeen. Kate, of course, had to think about what she needed, but she was also curious about what the girls needed so that "home" would feel like everyone's home and not that they were just living in Kate's home. Kate could guess what she thought they needed, but it's important to ask the question. Kate will never forget what Anna said: "I would really love my own set of keys." Awesome, Kate could do that!

Kate also asked for a couple of things that she needed: her office was on the same floor as their bedrooms, so she needed it to be quiet between 8 a.m. and 4 p.m. Kate also has a thing about a clean kitchen. The kitchen was theirs to do what they needed, but please wash up. Kate knew she would be so annoyed if she came down and they had made a mess in the kitchen and had not cleaned up. She needed to make that request obvious, to ask for what she wanted. And guess what? To this day they have never had an argument about the kitchen. Not one.

As you can imagine, different topics will come up in work environments. Depending on who you are working with, the topics will change. If you are having this conversation with a direct report, let them know what works for you and what doesn't, and ask the same of them. Topics might include:

- **One-on-ones:** what to expect, who owns the agenda, timing, who comes prepared for what

- **Calendaring:** what works and what doesn't

- **Feedback:** both how you want to receive it and how you want to give it

- **Communication:** preferences, modalities and turnaround time

- **Pet peeves:** name those little things that annoy you

Better Relationships

Too often, relationships begin at work or in life without pausing to clarify what each person needs. As you embark on a new project, arrangement or endeavor with another human, ask:

- What are we trying to achieve?
- What does success look like?
- Who is responsible for what?
- What does each of us need?
- How will we navigate roadblocks or conflict?
- What do we each want from this experience?

_____

_____

_____

_____

_____

_____

_____

_____

The trick is that this is not a one-time conversation. Together, you will need to revisit it, especially as situations change:

- How are we doing on these shared agreements?
- What needs to be modified?
- What is missing?

You are training the people around you how to treat you, all the time. Shared agreements are a key skill to be clear with others about how to treat you, in order for them to get the best from you and for you to get the best from them. This skill creates accountability and makes roles clear. It goes both ways and benefits the individuals and the whole organization immensely.

The fundamental shift is from being unconscious of your impact to taking ownership of the impact you create. The impact is happening and it's important to notice whether it was intended or unintended and to take responsibility. In this scenario, your shared agreements are with yourself, and knowledge is key, forming a structure for personal accountability.

Mindset Shift: Meaningful Connections

Healthy relationships, ones where people feel supported, require continuous attention. When you become complacent, take the relationship for granted or fail to take responsibility for your impact, meaningful connection will suffer. Power and status create an impact of their own, one that you as a leader need to be aware of.

Leadership is lonely. We know that might sound odd to those aspiring to the destination, but it is. You can no longer be "just one of the gang." Motives, yours and theirs, are called into question, competing demands create pressure and saying no can make you unpopular. Bearing the weight of it all, many leaders find it simpler to distance themselves from others. Leadership is nothing if people won't follow you. Leader isolation is real, and overcoming it centers on generating meaningful connections.[11]

Debbie was working with a project team made up predominantly of engineers, most of whom had decades of tenure at the company. A new VP had been hired from outside the organization, and he promptly went about running the unit and making decisions to move the company's business forward with greater speed and efficiency. The team of engineers were not happy with the "new guy." What the new VP thought was efficiency and taking control was experienced by the team as hubris: "Who was he to come in and take action without even the decency to ask or listen to our opinion on things before making big changes or commitments that affect us?" The new VP clearly was having an unintended impact on the team.

Meaningful connections are formed when people feel safe to admit when things are not going well. Once insights were gathered by the HR business partner and shared back, the new VP was mortified by how others were experiencing him. To his credit, he took responsibility for the impact he had created and immediately began to shift his lens from thinking about himself and what he needed to get done to building greater connections with the team. An accelerant to helping build a more trusted working relationship was the shared agreements they created to guide how they would work together going forward.

A happy side note to this story: as the new VP began to change, so did others around him. While the engineers were initially hesitant to speak up, with some clear ground rules for working together and a leader open to owning his impact, greater trust was built and the team flourished. Expanding your self-view to incorporate how others experience you and taking responsibility for the effect you have on those around you will lead to deeper, more meaningful connections.

Witnessing

We have referenced witnessing several times already in the book. It is one of our favorite skills. We could not close this chapter without sharing it with you. It both deepens the connection you have with someone and helps them understand the impact they create.

For Kate, this brings to mind her dad. He was an amazing champion of hers and a master of witnessing Kate and her growth as a woman in business. He was her biggest fan and greatest confidant. He would ask her questions and marvel at how she had handled one situation or other. He would not try to tell her what he would do, but rather would simply witness how she had decided to handle the situation. We could all follow this example of witnessing someone while giving them the space to grow, to try and to fail and succeed. To simply stand back and bear witness, paying attention, is a stance that can allow for amazing things to happen.

Debbie was interviewing candidates for an office manager role. A final question posed to each interviewee was "What are your pet peeves and why?" The reason for this question is that it hints at what is important to the person and aspects of their character. This particular interviewee answered, "When people judge me before they get to know me." The interviewee had pink hair and piercings in various parts of her face, things Debbie later learned her mother had told her to get rid of before the interview. Her heart stolen and curiosity piqued, Debbie dove deeper into the dialogue, which revealed a great deal more about the person's character. Debbie asked questions like: "What is important about that for you?" "Is there anything else I should know about that?" Debbie was simultaneously witnessing this candidate and learning more about what was important to her. This conversation created space for them to get to know one another and what was important. Together they determined they had the right chemistry to work together. As Debbie forwarded the candidate along in the interview process, she encouraged her to show up as the most honest reflection of herself. Anything less would deprive the candidate and the people she would be working with of an opportunity to form a true, meaningful relationship.

Like so much of what we are offering up, this is a shift in your awareness. What if you stopped trying to know more than others, or be better than others, all the time? What if you consciously decided to step into the practice of witnessing the people around you to see what they do, how they do it differently from you or better than you? Pause—and witness! Here is where breakthroughs can happen. Here is where meaningful connections are ignited.

7

daring not to know

DARING NOT TO KNOW is the practice of surrender. When you can accept that you do not know everything, and that others in the room know things you do not, you surrender. Surrender is magic because it creates connection; it can create safety and a sense that we are all in this together. This practice requires courage because admitting that you do not know is vulnerable work. Daring not to know takes strength and confidence to appreciate that things will be better when more ideas are included, when fuller representation is present and diverse perspectives are heard. Daring not to know paves the path to creating deeper engagement and loyalty from all your stakeholders: teammates, peers, colleagues and direct reports. You create space for them to step up, participate and inform the way forward. This sends a message that they are trusted and valued. In this practice, *you lead the way*.

Imagine This

It is dark. You are blindfolded and holding on to a rope. You have no idea what is about to happen. You know you are in a maze, but you do not know the way out. And you need to get out. You are told: "You are on the Path of Success. Many of the obstacles you encounter could be similar to those encountered on your own path to success in life. If you fail, it is because you forgot to live by the principles that overcome these obstacles. Along your journey, you will encounter people moving in different directions and at different speeds of confidence. Please be gentle in your journey."

And, of course, there are rules:

- Your goal is to find the door to success, which is how you exit the maze.
- You may not speak, except to ask for help.
- You may not let go of the rope, duck under or climb over the rope, or untie any knot.

You begin to move. You are looking for the way out. It is here. You know it is here and you need to find it. You are bumping into other people and obstacles—Was that a tree? You know if you work hard enough you will find the exit. You ask, "Am I close?" Your question goes unanswered; the rules are simply repeated. You keep moving along the rope, determined to find the door to success. Notice:

- What are you feeling?
- What stories are you telling yourself?
- What are your saboteurs telling you?
- How will you get out of here?[1]

This leadership development exercise, initially created by Tom Courry, is, of course, a metaphor for your life. As we are writing this, we are in the middle of a pandemic. None of us knows how this global crisis will play out and most of us are frantically looking for the "door to success." Some of us are stumbling along with cautious steps, while others are fixed in place, unable to move forward. We want to get on with it. Exactly what "it" will be, no one really knows.

What is it like to say "I don't know" as a leader? Often your own fears will not let you utter those words. There is pressure

"Life is about not knowing,
having to change, taking
the moment and making the
best of it, without knowing
what is going to happen next."

GILDA RADNER

to know, to decide, to look confident and composed. Somewhere along the way, you got the societal message that, as a leader, you needed to "know" when, in fact, you cannot know everything all the time. How do you decide when you do not know? One option is to gather insights from others, realizing it is a tough balance between needing to make a decision and listening to the input from the people around you.

The explosion of the *Challenger* space shuttle on January 28, 1986, is a perfect example of the balance being off. Bob Ebeling, an engineer who worked for the company that produced the booster, had cautioned that the extremely cold weather would stop the O-rings from sealing the way they were supposed to and would cause an explosion. Writer Elizabeth Anderson explains, "He and another engineer then requested that the shuttle's launch be delayed until the weather was favorable. The delay was initially granted but was later dismissed by executives, who were under pressure to get the shuttle into space, as the launch had already been delayed six days."[2] Unfortunately, seventy-three seconds after takeoff, the *Challenger* exploded, and all seven astronauts were killed.

For leaders, what gets in the way of really hearing the warning signs that others are signaling? In the article "Predictable Surprises," Michael Watkins and Max Bazerman state that predictable surprises take many forms, from financial scandals to disruptions in operations, from organizational upheavals to product failures. Some result in short-term losses or distractions, while others cause damage that takes years to repair.[3] Watkins and Bazerman examine the avoidable organizational barriers that get in the way, such as communication and information flow, psychological issues like biased decision making, and special interest groups that have too much clout. In the case of the *Challenger*, we may never know what could have happened if people had been able to hear the warning signals.

It's critical to admit that you do not know everything. That admission invites people to participate and share what they know. It will help you move out of your own preconceived biases. Reaching out to the people alongside you to help navigate the complex decisions you have in front of you will be your secret weapon.

You do not have to know everything! In fact, it is impossible. Yet so much of corporate and organizational life has you pretending that you know things when you do not. You are at best using logic and at worst fearful to decide at all. In some respects, you have to proceed without knowing, to stretch yourself into learning. Most people are promoted into jobs, stretching into roles they have never done before, shadowed by the ever-present imposter syndrome. Imposter syndrome can be defined as "feelings of inadequacy that persist despite evident success."[4] When you are young, you need to prove your know-how. As you progress in your career, and as you begin to acquire a team, things change. The problems are undoubtedly more complex, and engagement becomes a greater concern. How do you engage the people around you without feeling less-than? By daring not to know.

Many folks will push back on this, saying, "I need to, at minimum, look like I know what is going on, or we might be getting into the realm of ineffectiveness." But this is where the magic of daring not to know comes in. When you are working with other people, this practice ignites participation. Surprisingly, it does the opposite of what you might expect: you may fear it will make you look ineffective or, worse, inept, but instead it creates a safe place for people to be courageous. You lead the way by letting go, and space opens up for others to offer what they know.

Each of our internal worlds is vast and holds information and insight to be mined. Kevin Cashman writes about this so eloquently in his book *Leadership from the Inside Out*: "Few people would admit that they know everything *outside* themselves. We all understand how unfathomable external knowledge and information is. We see the external world as huge. Our inner life, however, is defined too often in a very restricted way... There are no limits within us... It is bigger, deeper, and grander that the external world we think is so vast."[5]

Your job as a leader is to mine your own internal world and the worlds of the people around you. Because they may have the key that unlocks the door you need to open.

Connecting Engagement and Productivity

In chapter 5, we said alignment is about the head. Engagement, then, is all about the heart. According to Imaginasium, "It's emotional—and it's directly focused on how people *feel* about where things are going, whether they agree, how they react to what's being asked of them and whether they care enough to give it their all."[6] Who doesn't want that in their organization? Engagement is the golden elixir for productivity.

According to Gallup, highly engaged teams are 21 percent more productive than those with low engagement. Engaged employees are innovative; they always have an idea or two about what they can improve.[7] Productivity is what they get done. Engagement is how they feel while they do it. Two very different things. Tony Boatman writes in his article "How Employee Engagement and Productivity Are Related": "Engaged employees are those invested in the firm and their work. They're the ones who speak up in meetings, who want to know more about what the company does and why it does it. They're the ones who actively think about the firm's

processes—and how things can be improved. They're commu-
nicative, and they bring enthusiasm to their work."[8] Boatman
continues that they are creative thinkers, collaborative and
efficient, and have strong work ethics, which all lead to better
productivity.

And engaged employees means better quality productivity. In the article "How Employee Engagement Drives Growth,"
Susan Sorenson states: "Work units in the top quartile in
employee engagement outperformed bottom-quartile units
by 10% on customer ratings, 22% in profitability, and 21% in
productivity."[9] Of course, these units also saw a drop in turnover, absenteeism, safety issues and quality issues. Just as
research shows that unproductive employees can cost your
firm money,[10] research also shows that engaged employees *are*
productive employees. It's easy to see why: engaged employees
want to be involved and informed. They bring more energy to
their work, along with a more positive attitude.[11] Engagement
is about more than productivity. Engagement is about people's
hearts and feelings and enthusiasm. This is productivity on
steroids. Who doesn't want to tap into that?

So, how do you incite engagement? Create space for others, appreciating that they will know more than you about
some topics. It takes courage to know that things will improve
when more ideas are included, when representation is broad
and diverse perspectives are heard. When you can confidently
stand in a space of daring not to know, you invite others into
the conversation. This is bold!

A leader who dares not to know turns the limited idea
that you need to know everything into the liberating concept
that you need to mine the people around you for what they
see and know. Be curious. What are their ideas? What do they
see that you do not? How might they contribute to everyone's
learning? It takes vulnerability to admit that you do not know.

When you accept that you do not know everything, and that others in the room know things you do not, you surrender.

Our culture tends to reward those who know—and by gosh, if we don't, we will make it up! This creates insincerity—the opposite of vulnerability. Admitting that you don't know does not mean you are not smart. It simply creates an invitation for others to step in to bring their brilliance. In other words, it creates engagement.

How Daring Not to Know Fosters Engagement

"Engagement" is a buzzword these days. Everyone wants it. It seems to be the lost Atlantis of the corporate world. If only...! Peter Cappelli and Liat Eldor's argument in their article "Where Measuring Engagement Goes Wrong" is that one of the primary reasons engagement studies are ineffective is because there is no universal definition of engagement. Multiple definitions abound, measuring vigor, passion, pride and enthusiasm for work, or contributing to the company's success, or satisfaction.[12]

At HumanityWorks, when we speak of engagement, we mean whether people care about their work and the organization they work for. We look at their discretionary effort, whether they go above and beyond because they are engaged in your cause. They believe in what you are doing and why you are doing it. And they believe that they have a role to play in the organization attaining that goal. In other words, they want to contribute. This is your sweet spot and it's a challenge to achieve. Engaging your people is a superpower, your hidden advantage.

One way to foster engagement is by asking questions, lots of questions. In his book *The Coaching Habit*, Michael Bungay Stanier refers to the work of academic Paul Nutt, who studied 168 decisions made within organizations. "He found that in 71 percent of the decisions, the choice preceding the decision was binary. It was simply: Should we do this? Or should we not?"[13] The failure rate of those decisions was more than 50 percent. However, by adding a third option (Should we do this, or that, or should we not?) that rate dropped to 30 percent. As a leader, ask open-ended questions and resist binary options.

Inviting participation

Daring not to know paves the path to deeper engagement and loyalty from all your stakeholders: teammates, peers, colleagues and direct reports. You create space for them to step up, participate and inform the way forward. This sends a message that they are trusted and valued. By doing this, you, my friend, are leading the way. You are modeling the impact that you want to have.

Dare not to know, dare to open up to a new perspective, and even dare to see the power of what a team "doing the work of their life" can do. Joan Burke, chief people officer of Docu-Sign, says her work with the Five Practices encouraged her to see that work is deeply personal and meaningful, not only to herself but also to her team members. And because of this realization, she now leads by framing issues more courageously and with the trust needed to allow others to step in. "We look at issues in a way that helps shift perspectives, but in a non-threatening way," says Joan. "Our motto at DocuSign is 'doing the work of your life.'"

Joan's leadership allows her people to step into that concept—that the work of your life is personal as well as professional—a vulnerable but powerful stance. "We now encourage each other to broaden the point of view when facing a challenge and think in an entirely different way. To be bold and innovative. To turn things on their head and examine it from a new perspective." Giving up the need to know, the need to be right, the DocuSign culture encourages innovation. New viewpoints are sought out and listened to. "This allows the team to see their better selves and be more creative in getting to the root of an issue. It helps team members get unstuck—but in a super-caring way helps them feel very special and valued and heard."[14]

Leaders who dare to say "I don't know" are in good company. At a 2017 Presidential Leadership Scholars series, former presidents Bill Clinton and George W. Bush both spoke about the most important quality for being a president. What was that premier quality? Knowledge? Intelligence? Leadership skills? Experience? Nope. It was humility. Both presidents stressed the virtue of humility. "'I think it's really important to know what you don't know and listen to people who do know what you don't know,' Bush said. Clinton... agreed that officeholders need to be humble, and warned that those 'who are real arrogant in office' have forgotten that history will be their judge."[15]

In fact, the need for leaders to say "I don't know" took on urgent importance for many companies during the fast-changing health and economic effects of the pandemic crisis of 2020. As the authors of the *Harvard Business Review* article "4 Behaviors That Help Leaders Manage a Crisis" note, "strong leaders get ahead of changing circumstances. They seek input and information from diverse sources, are not afraid to admit what they don't know, and bring in outside expertise when needed."[16] The American Psychological Association backs this up, saying that leaders need to use credibility to build trust when times are uncertain: "Credibility is a combination of expertise and dependability. Leaders gain credibility when they demonstrate that they understand the risks and ramifications of a situation. At the same time, leaders should not expect that they know all the answers. Good leaders admit when they don't know the answer to a question and defer to other experts."[17]

And somewhere along the way, the idea spread that leaders need to "know," that it is a sign of "weakness" if you do not know everything—which we all realize, in the clear light of day, is impossible. VUCA is a concept originated with students at the US Army War College to describe the volatility, uncertainty, complexity and ambiguity of the world after the Cold War. And now, the concept has gained new relevance to characterize the current fast-changing business environment and the leadership required to navigate it successfully. This term is spilling over into our everyday lives, too. We live in an age when the problems we are trying to solve, the things we are bringing into existence, require a new level of participation. You simply cannot know everything all the time.

There is technical intelligence—what you do and know; and there is emotional intelligence—how you go about it. Daniel Goleman, author of *Emotional Intelligence*, writes that 15 percent of what you do every day is technical knowledge, and 85 percent is emotional intelligence.[18] You have technical knowledge or experience that is completely relevant. So much of what you do beyond this is reliant upon your emotional intelligence—the soft skills. Curiosity is one of those skills.

Core Skill: Curiosity

Curiosity is defined by the *Merriam-Webster* dictionary as a desire to know, inquisitive interest in the concerns of others (even nosiness!), and interest leading to inquiry (as in, intellectual curiosity). Curiosity is the antidote to judgment. It is expressed through powerful questions that provoke deeper thinking, yielding new insights and discoveries.

Curiosity and powerful questions are superskills, and we have referenced their superpowers many times in this book. They broaden the landscape. They expand information, connection, participation. The skill of curiosity deepens what you know and can challenge your assumptions.

Daring not to know means practicing the power of curiosity to create deeper engagement. What would our workplaces be like if each of us had the willingness to stay curious about things, in particular with others' opinions and behaviors that are different from our own? Not just for the sport of it, but to genuinely seek understanding, to remain open rather than letting our sense of righteousness or the duality of judgment creep in. *I am right and you are wrong.* This old narrative keeps you small, protecting how you see the world.

Curiosity expands information, connection, participation. It deepens what you know and can challenge what you think you knew. Becoming conscious about your own curiosity is the first step in expanding your awareness, going from what you alone know to mining the riches of what they know!

When you practice curiosity, you stand in an open posture, ready to listen and receive what is said, without judgment. The skills of listening at levels 2 and 3 are prerequisites to curiosity. Paying attention to the other and to the environment as a whole, you can ascertain what is really happening and access different truths and potential connection.

One big roadblock to curiosity is time. People are stretched so thin that pausing to see and get curious about the people around them becomes an obstacle. When you are pushing on a deadline, taking time to gather input from others might seem like a time suck, so you zoom right past any opportunity to gather new insights or ideas.

Truly opening up to another's ideas can be distracting and sometimes unsettling, so you hunker down and stay the course. Instead, try to pause, and take a moment to listen to others with curiosity—it is the key that opens new possibilities you probably wouldn't have seen if you'd rushed by. If you start your day with more curiosity, you might unlock something surprising from the people around you: more ideas, more connection, more innovation, more collaboration.

A second roadblock is knowing what to do with the input you receive from those unlocked people. Flooded with new insights and information, you may ask, "Now what?" Ultimately, you need to determine what has value and what is not useful at the moment—but that is a good problem to have.

We gained an insightful image about the importance of curiosity during a conversation with the CEO of a company we were working with. As requested, we had been providing regular updates to the executive team about a project we were leading. Wanting to ensure we were adding value, we asked the CEO if these updates were beneficial or if they were merely noise in his airways. He commented that each update was like a piece of mosaic tile, and when combined they created a picture for him that he would not have been able to see otherwise. All the little pieces that make up the big picture—that is what curiosity can unearth.

Curiosity holds the door open for others to walk in. You invite people in to share what they see and know and imagine. Rather than casting not knowing as a weakness, you offer it up as an invitation to co-create.

Better Curiosity

Curiosity and the use of powerful questions will help you develop depth and mastery in building engagement. Powerful questions are the driving force in the cadence of inquiry. We offer a few for you to use during the initial process of daring not to know. Ask yourself, and ask others:

- What do I/you think?
- What do I/you mean by that?
- What's important about that?
- What are we missing?
- What is obvious but we are not seeing it?
- What do you see that I am not seeing?
- If we were not afraid, what would we do?
- What else?

Mindset Shift: Outcome-Creating

Outcome-creating is the mindset that enables you to step into a situation and actively create the outcome you want or generate something new. You are focused on the possibility in the challenge rather than viewing the situation as a problem. The desired outcome creates the energy that propels you forward.

Kate once led a group in which a participant in the session forever changed her. Now, this is a common by-product of her work. She is inspired and changed by the people in the rooms that she co-leads all the time. But this session was different. This participant was different.

She was working for an organization that told her and her co-leader that a man who was differently abled would be attending their session. They said his physical needs hadn't been a problem in past sessions but, if they had any questions, to contact them.

Before the day's session began, Kate and her co-leader, Jenny, choreographed the first demonstration of the class, which required a participant to move around a circle describing different aspects of what they were thinking and feeling. Jenny and Kate agreed that Kate would coach the participant as they experienced the model and that Jenny would, in essence, narrate what was going on. Soon, the group arrived, including the man, Brad, in his wheelchair, along with his wife. Jenny and Kate introduced themselves to Brad and his wife and learned that he had cerebral palsy. When he spoke, his speech was difficult for Kate and Jenny to understand. His wife cheerily told the two facilitators that she would be leaving. They both paused, noticing they were far out of their comfort zones and uncertain how to make this interactive and experiential course accessible for him, for others and for themselves.

Soon it was time to begin the class, and Kate and Jenny asked the room, "Who has an issue that they are struggling with and need some help?" For Kate, it was like a scene out of a movie; the room dimmed and a light shone on Brad. No one else raised a hand. Kate said, "Okay, Brad, come on up." She had no idea how the exercise was going to work. Then the magic happened. As they began working on Brad's issue, and as Kate let go of a need to know, something opened up. Sometimes she understood him and could move the demonstration forward, and sometimes she could not understand him but someone else in the room could. Sometimes no one else could understand Brad and so they asked him to try again. All the while, something palpably bigger was going on. Although it was not a conscious choice, Kate had surrendered to the opportunity that was in front of everyone in the room, and together they *all* created an amazing learning situation. They could do it, when they did it together.

So often, we think ten steps ahead. As Jenny and Kate talked later, they realized that sometimes you just need to slow down, surrender, dare not to know, and do the one thing in front of you that needs to be done. Then the next thing. And so on. One step at a time.

Can you see the outcome-creating mindset in this example? The shift for Kate and Jenny was in daring not to know and letting go. It was in pausing and asking for more input. They led the way by creating the invitation for others to participate, and, in turn, people felt valued.

Step up and do better

During one of our programs in Silicon Valley, a cohort of directors was in the habit of complaining about what the executive team was not doing or should be doing. One of the activities we designed was for some of the executive team to do an open question-and-answer session with the cohort. We prepared some questions for the executives about their own path of leadership, and we also planned to open questions up to the room.

Let go of the idea that you own the burden and **step into the belief that together you can achieve more.**

When we did, some directors were very direct in asking the executive team members about certain business decisions or indecisions. To the surprise of most of the directors, the executives admitted that they were simply making the best decisions they could with the information they had—and that a great deal of that information came from the director level. There was no omniscience or magic to these decisions. Most of the executive team admitted that—like for everyone else—a lot is made it up as they go along.

We, who had designed this training, sat back and watched the lightbulbs go on for this group of directors. They realized that the executives were people just like them and that, in fact, they needed the directors. This open conversation helped the directors feel valued and also liberated to use their knowledge and common sense to take on more responsibilities. It gave them permission to step up, lead the way and take real ownership. As a result, this group of directors grew into leaders. This is the goal of so many organizations: to engage people so that they step up to solve the organization's problems and move forward.

Sometimes daring not to know comes as a revelation. A couple of years ago we were doing some work with an organization that was merging with another company. Leaders from each company knew little to nothing about each other, so a key objective was their getting to know one another as humans. The activities of the day were to help them interact with one another openly, honestly, even vulnerably. And life showed up! At the end of a very intense day, we were in the elevator with the CEO. We will never forget what he said with genuine amazement: "Man, you forget that people have lives outside of work." Wow. That was a big moment of clarity for him. You can forget this at times—you think of the people as the job that they are doing and whether they are helping you or getting in your way.

Herein lies a nuanced middle ground. How can you show up for what you need to do, but also allow yourself to be honest about what is going on for you? Can you expand to include both your ability to get the job done and have room for the vulnerability to not know?

Problem-reacting is often driven by the belief that you need to solve problems by yourself. Outcome-creating is letting go of the idea that you own the burden to solve problems on your own and stepping into the belief that together you can achieve more. People join companies because they want to be a part of something bigger than themselves. You create shared purpose by opening up space for them to meaningfully engage in the journey. And in the space of daring not to know, you will discover new things.

For most of us, this level of vulnerability can be uncomfortable. Especially in a work setting, where we have this script running through our heads that tells us we must be strong, we must not crack, others are depending on us, we must know all the answers—and whatever other of your favorite reasons you care to fill in. Author Brené Brown talks about the power of vulnerability.[19] At its core, this is a belief that you are worthy of love, of being cared for. Surrounding you are friends, allies and mentors to help. Whenever you need it. The thing you need the most, you are often hesitant to seek. And the odd thing is, the hands and hearts are always there. Don't hesitate to ask for help. This will serve you well in work and in life.

Back to the Maze and the Rope

It is dark. You are blindfolded and holding on to a rope. You have no idea what is about to happen. You know you are in a maze, but you do not know the way out. And you need to get out. You are told: "You are on the Path of Success. Many of the obstacles you encounter could be similar to those encountered on your own path to success in life. If you fail it is because you forget to live by the principles that overcome these obstacles. Along your journey, you will encounter people moving in different directions and at different speeds of confidence. Please be gentle in your journey."

And of course, there are rules:

- Your goal is to find the door to success, which is how you exit the maze.
- You may not speak, except to ask for help.
- You may not let go of the rope, duck under or climb over the rope, or untie any knot.

You begin to move. You are looking for the way out. It is here. You know it is here and you need to find it. You are bumping into other people and obstacles—Was that a tree? You just know that if you work hard enough you will find the exit. You ask, "Am I close?" Your questions goes unanswered; the rules are simply repeated. You keep moving along the rope. You *will* find the "door to success."

Suddenly, you pause. You realize that you have gone around and around and cannot get out. You ask for help. Someone is immediately by your side. "Do you want help?" they ask, their voice full of compassion. "Yes," you reply. They say, "Congratulations, by asking for help you have found the door to success." And you are free.[20]

conclusion
imagine this

IMAGINE YOU ARE focused on the project at hand, one with a looming deadline that requires your undivided attention. Your boss sends a notification via Slack that she needs to speak with you right away—the message is void of any context or background. You are startled by its briskness and immediately stop what you are doing. Walking into the meeting, you can tell from her posture and her agitation that she is wound up about something. She launches into what is on her mind. Your own mind races to catch up to hers. As her long-winded narrative, still void of much context or background, comes to a close, she comments, "I just need this done and done right now."

You turn to leave the room, your head still spinning to make sense of what just happened. Whatever it was, your boss has some clear idea that you just need to do the work, without question or dialogue. You sit wondering about this opaque conversation, what "it" looks like and, more importantly, how you are going to get this mystery work done along with your looming project deadline. You feel yourself reeling, reacting. You start hammering out an email to your team. You'll meet before noon to reprioritize the week's work. But before you hit send, you pause, take a breath. Your boss's reactive state does not mean you need to be triggered into yours. You can make this work better, for yourself and for her. You can do this.

You send her a note, letting her know you have a few questions and ideas about the conversation and need a few minutes of her time. She agrees to meet, and in the meeting you lead with curiosity, asking a series of powerful questions that help both of you understand what "it" could look like. You receive the much-needed clarity on what it will take to realize the request. You understand more about her needs, so you can ask for her help prioritizing this new request alongside the other project deadline. You learn that this request can wait a few days until your immediate deadline is done. (You are a hero for saving your team from an unnecessary all-nighter!) Focused and grounded, albeit with one more thing on your to-do list, you leave the room. You might have lost a half-hour, but in the long run you saved a lot more. And you strengthened the relationship between you and your boss. You've got this!

Different things are going on for your boss. After the second meeting, she pauses for a minute and reflects on what just happened, for her, for you and for your working relationship. She realizes that when she first reached out to you, she was pretty wound up. She had not intended to create such a whirlwind, and she was grateful you were able to stop the swirl before a ton of precious time, energy and money was spent in a very unproductive way. Her learning: take a beat and breathe before creating chaos and unnecessary work for the team. She experienced the power of pausing, for just a moment or two, and of asking a few grounding questions before jumping hair-on-fire into the doing of work. It clarified the outcome she was trying to create and the problem she was trying to solve.

She also realizes how helpful your questions were. They made her stop and consider things more deeply and helped focus the issue: what was important and why. It was so helpful to be asked, "What are we solving for and how will we know when it is achieved?" Lastly, she notes the ease with which the two of you navigated those hurdles. You pushed back, but you did it in such a respectful and helpful manner that it was productive. You were a team, at ease in the conversation, and that made it easy to create the right outcome.

While it was tough in the moment, standing in the mess let you both grow. You are constantly training the people around you how to treat you, and this moment was a great reminder that when you change, the people around you also begin to change.

Humanity Works Better

At the risk of sounding like a script from a Hallmark Channel special, here's a dirty little secret: sometimes your efforts to bring more humanity to work will work out and sometimes they won't. And you will never know unless you are willing to step up and try to make work better for yourself and those around you. *Humanity Works Better* is about navigating the reality of your situation. It is not a magic pill. It is not a playbook. It is not a collection of leadership platitudes. It is a book for you, a perfectly imperfect human who leads others by navigating the complex and true realities of work. And this is hard, messy work. *Humanity Works Better* is about how to become more aware of yourself, to step into a different choice about how to be with others and to have the courage to change and try something different.

You now have a toolkit of practices and skills to help you get the most from the people around you. You can make productivity all about your people. The Five Practices will help you become stronger as you use them, test them, modify them and make them your own. As you use them more and more, they will become second nature to you, like riding a bike. Working with others with agility, grace and humanity will become a strength. Leadership is a practice, a muscle to be built. And it starts with you.

We are here to help and support your journey. At Humanity-Works, we are on a mission to bring more humanity into the workplace and fundamentally change the world of work. (See the last pages of this book to learn more about our offerings.) Let your journey begin!

Where to Begin?

- **Start with awareness:** Where are you stuck, and what mind-set shift would serve you best right now?
- **Exercise choice:** Choose a skill from the Five Practices, one you feel drawn to and that is challenging enough to stretch you out of your comfort zone.
- **Have courage:** Begin . . . just begin. You will not be perfect at this. Keep working it! When you change, those around you will too.
- **Begin again:** Your growth and potential is never-ending.

_____

_____

_____

_____

_____

_____

_____

acknowledgments

RITING A BOOK is such a heady exercise. You have to think really hard about what you want to say, how to say it and why it's important to say it. And for us, it is also a heart exercise. It is about what we believe and what we want to bring into the world. Lucky us—we had the chance to do it together.

This book has been decades in the making, and there are so many people who contributed to it and to our work on it, and the work that contributed to it. We are forever grateful to you.

Challengers: Mihca Anderson, Anika Briner, Dino Anderson and Amie Fitzhugh are our Dream Team. This crew called us forward, dared us to quit playing small and to fully step into our greatest potential. You have championed and challenged us every step of the way. You are our people. We love you for seeing us and wanting more from us. You made us play bigger.

Way-shower: Sue Barlow of Barlow Initiatives. There are so many archetypes Sue fits into for us: champion, coach, friend, way-shower. She showed us the way to create this book, all with an unwavering, steady hand. She guided us from a myriad of sticky-note ideas and our shitty first draft to a manuscript submitted for publication. She showed us the way, encouraging and championing us every step along this journey. We could not have done this without her.

Pioneers: Athena Katsaros for her deep value and belief in this work. Athena had her sleeves rolled up and contributed to the early formation of ideas in our work at Mozilla. The kernels planted more than a decade ago have bloomed into this thinking. Jeff Jacobson, you brought humor and light to our ideas and made the doing of this work with clients come to life.

Warriors: Our spouses, George and Josh, for their unflinching support of our wild and ambitious vision to bring more humanity to the workplace and fundamentally change the world of work. You nurture our souls with your unconditional love.

Guardians: The Page Two team provided us with nurturing guidance and compassionate discipline—and they are so much fun to work with. We are indebted to Jesse Finkelstein, co-founder of Page Two, for believing in us; and to Kendra Ward, our editor, for making our words become the dog-eared reference tool we imagined it could be. We are grateful to Peter Cocking, who gave creative expression and life to our words; to Tilman Lewis, for meticulously wordsmithing our manuscript; to Chris Brandt, for leading the marketing efforts to expand our reach; to Lorraine Toor and her sales team, for placing our books on so many shelves in both literal and figurative ways; and to Caela Moffet, for tirelessly orchestrating every detail to turn our early manuscript into the book you now hold in your hands.

Shapeshifters: The multitude of people who have participated in our workshops, leadership programs and coaching—we are endlessly inspired by your adaptability, reinvention and transformation. A special shout-out to those who participated in our research interviews: Jim Cook, Kate Naszradi, Andreas Gal, Debbie Shotwell, Dino Anderson, Mihca Anderson, Amie Fitzhugh, Anika Briner, Pete Scanlon, Ben Adida, Laura Owen, Veronique Rozen, Laura Spencer, Tom Cignarella and, in particular, those who allowed their voices to join ours in creating this book: Jane Finette, Pascal Finette, Tyler Bosmeny, Ryan Merkley, Mary Colvig, Ben Limmer, Joan Burke, Leland Franklin, Angela Kiniry and Billy Kilmer.

Advocates: The boundless interest and support from our numerous friends and family has encouraged and inspired us—there are so many of you. A special shout-out to Brady, Michelle, Bryan and Melissa. You were always there, checking in on us, showing interest in our work, lending a hand to read a passage, test an idea or enrich our thinking. Your quiet, consistent championing of this project kept us going in ways you will never fully know, and we are eternally grateful for each of you.

Artist: Jennah Synnestvedt of Soulful Brand, who helped capture the essence of our brand, even as we were creating it and didn't always know what it should look like. Jennah realized our vision.

Muses: Co-Active Training Institute, to Henry and Karen Kimsey-House for their inspiration and willingness to share their insights and knowledge with us and the world. The Leadership Circle for creating a visionary tool that is so accessible and transformational and for granting us the permission to share the magic of it with others. There are so many other people cited in this book who inspire our thinking and continuously challenge us to bring more humanity to the workplace.

True Believers: Mozilla, where our partnership was born, and our clients leading the way of being human-centered organizations: Clever, Charge EPC, Articulate, Pinterest.

notes

Introduction

1 "Productivity and Accountability," 21st Century Skills, sites.google.com/
   site/twentyfirststcenturyskills/analysis.

1: Productivity—It's All About People

1 Michael Mankins, "Great Companies Obsess Over Productivity, Not Efficiency," *Harvard Business Review*, March 1, 2017, hbr.org/2017/03/great
   -companies-obsess-over-productivity-not-efficiency.
2 Alexia Fernández Campbell, "The US Is Experiencing a Widespread
   Worker Shortage. Here's Why." Vox, March 18, 2019, vox.com/2019/3/18/
   18270916/labor-shortage-workers-us; "Job Openings and Labor Turnover Summary," Economic News Release, US Bureau of Labor Statistics,
   December 9, 2020, bls.gov/news.release/jolts.nr0.htm.
3 Marilyn Price-Mitchell, "Teaching Civility in an F-Word Society," *Psychology Today*, June 23, 2012, psychologytoday.com/us/blog/the-moment
   -youth/201206/teaching-civility-in-f-word-society.
4 Christine Porath, *Mastering Civility: A Manifesto for the Workplace* (New
   York: Grand Central Publishing, 2016).
5 Gary Namie, *2017 U.S. Workplace Bullying Study* (Clarkston, WA: Workplace
   Bullying Institute, 2017), workplacebullying.org/download/2017-wbi/.
6 Baron Christopher Hanson, "Diagnose and Eliminate Workplace Bullying," *Harvard Business Review*, July 13, 2011, hbr.org/2011/07/diagnose
   -and-eliminate-workplace.
7 *State of the Global Workplace* (Washington, DC: Gallup, 2017), gallup.com/
   workplace/238079/state-global-workplace-2017.aspx; Susan Sorenson
   and Keri Garman, "How to Tackle U.S. Employees' Stagnating Engagement," Gallup, Business Journal, June 11, 2013, news.gallup.com/business
   journal/162953/tackle-employees-stagnating-engagement.aspx.

8 *State of the American Manager: Analytics and Advice for Leaders* (Washington, DC: Gallup, 2015), m100group.files.wordpress.com/2015/07/stateof americanmanager_0515_mh_lr.pdf.

9 Emma Seppälä and Kim Cameron, "Proof That Positive Work Cultures Are More Productive," *Harvard Business Review*, December 1, 2015, hbr.org/ 2015/12/proof-that-positive-work-cultures-are-more-productive.

10 Kim Cameron et al., "Effects of Positive Practices on Organizational Performance," *Journal of Applied Behavioral Science* 47, no. 3 (2011): 266– 308, doi.org/10.1177/0021886310395514; David S. Bright, Kim Cameron and Arran Caza, "The Amplifying and Buffering Effects of Virtuousness in Downsized Organizations," *Journal of Business Ethics* 64 (March 2006): 249–69, doi.org/10.1007/s10551-005-5904-4.

11 Seppälä and Cameron, "Proof That Positive Work Cultures Are More Productive."

12 Adam Grant, *Give and Take: Why Helping Others Drives Our Success* (New York: Penguin Books, 2013).

13 "Creating a Culture of Feedback at CHG Healthcare," DecisionWise, decision -wise.com/chg_healthcare.

14 Kevin McCoy, "Number of CEOs Who Exited after Bad Behavior Grows," *USA Today*, June 21, 2018, usatoday.com/story/money/2018/06/21/number -ceos-leaving-after-bad-behavior-grows/721025002.

15 Zoe Schiffer, "Emotional Baggage," Verge, December 5, 2019, theverge .com/2019/12/5/20995453/away-luggage-ceo-steph-korey-toxic-work -environment-travel-inclusion.

16 *The Financial Impact of a Positive Employee Experience* (Armonk, NY: IBM Smarter Workforce Institute/WorkHuman, 2018), ibm.com/downloads/ cas/XEY1K26O.

2: Shifting Your Mindset to Embrace Change

1 Carol Dweck, *Mindset: The New Psychology of Success* (New York: Ballantine Books, 2006), 4.

2 Carol Dweck quoted in "Mindsets," Peak Performance Center, thepeak performancecenter.com/development-series/mental-conditioning/ mindsets.

3 Dweck quoted in "Mindsets," Peak Performance Center.

4 "Mindsets," Peak Performance Center.

5 Robert Kegan and Lisa Laskow Lahey, *Immunity to Change: How to Overcome It and Unlock the Potential in Yourself and Your Organization* (Boston: Harvard Business School Publishing, 2009).

6 Bob Anderson, *The Leadership Circle: Breakthrough Leadership Assessment Technology* (Draper, UT: Leadership Circle, 2016), 2y3l3p1ohb5c1 lkzte2wv2ks-wpengine.netdna-ssl.com/wp-content/uploads/2018/03/ LCP_Breakthrough.pdf, 186.

7   For more on reactive tendencies, see Robert J. Anderson and William A. Adams, *Mastering Leadership: An Integrated Framework for Breakthrough Performance and Extraordinary Business Results* (Hoboken: John Wiley & Sons, 2016), 188.

8   See Leadership Circle's website for more information about its 360 tool at leadershipcircle.com/en/products/leadership-circle-profile/.

9   Lana Osborne-Paradis, "5 Words That Helped Me Finally Enforce My Boundaries," Blast Fitness, February 6, 2019, blastfitness.ca/mindset/5-words-helped-finally-enforce-boundaries.

10 Interview with Ben Limmer, solutions architect, Ibotta, conducted by Barlow Initiatives, November 2019.

11 *The Leadership Circle Profile Interpretation Manual*, version TLC 10.1 (Leadership Circle, n.d.), 13.

12 Interview with Angela Kiniry, VP of people, Articulate, conducted by Barlow Initiatives, February 2021.

3: Creating Safety

1   Paul J. Zak, "The Neuroscience of Trust," *Harvard Business Review*, January–February 2017, hbr.org/2017/01/the-neuroscience-of-trust.

2   Thomas F. Mahan et al., *2019 Retention Report: Trends, Reasons & A Call to Action* (Franklin, TN: Work Institute, 2019), info.workinstitute.com/hubfs/2019%20Retention%20Report/Work%20Institute%202019%20Retention%20Report%20final-1.pdf.

3   Robert C. Solomon and Fernando Flores, *Building Trust in Business, Politics, Relationships, and Life* (New York: Oxford University Press, 2001), 59–63.

4   Richard Fagerlin, "The Big Lie about Trust—5 Reasons Why Trust Is Not Earned," blog, May 2015, richardfagerlin.com/2015/05/the-big-lie-about-trust-5-reasons-why-trust-is-not-earned.

5   Fagerlin, "The Big Lie about Trust."

6   Amy Edmondson interview, "Creating Psychological Safety in the Workplace," *HBR IdeaCast* (podcast), Episode 666, January 22, 2019, hbr.org/podcast/2019/01/creating-psychological-safety-in-the-workplace.

7   Wikipedia, s.v., "Away (company)," en.wikipedia.org/wiki/Away_(luggage).

8   Schiffer, "Emotional Baggage."

9   Steven Melendez, "Away Luggage Hires Defamation Law Firm in Response to Article That Alleges Toxic Work Environment," *Fast Company*, January 13, 2020, fastcompany.com/90451365/away-luggage-hires-defamation-law-firm-in-response-to-article-that-alleged-toxic-work-environment.

10 Harlan Coben Quotations, *QuoteTab*, quotetab.com/quotes/by-harlan-coben.

11   Charles Duhigg, "What Google Learned from Its Quest to Build the Perfect Team," *New York Times Magazine*, February 25, 2016, nytimes .com/2016/02/28/magazine/what-google-learned-from-its-quest-to-build -the-perfect-team.html.
12   Duhigg, "What Google Learned."
13   Dennis Jaffe, "The Essential Importance of Trust: How to Build It or Restore It," *Forbes*, December 5, 2018, forbes.com/sites/dennisjaffe/2018/12/05/ the-essential-importance-of-trust-how-to-build-it-or-restore-it.
14   Interview, Ryan Merkley, chief of staff, Wikimedia Foundation, conducted by Barlow Initiatives, November 2019.
15   Adapted from Laura Whitworth et al., *Co-Active Coaching: The Proven Framework for Transformative Conversations at Work and in Life*, 2nd ed. (Mountain View, CA: Davies-Black Publishing, 2007).

4: Working Together

1   "The Global Economic Outlook during the COVID-19 Pandemic: A Changed World," World Bank, June 8, 2020, worldbank.org/en/news/ feature/2020/06/08/the-global-economic-outlook-during-the-covid-19 -pandemic-a-changed-world.
2   "New Study Reveals the Connection between Resilience and Positive Business Outcomes," meQuilibrium, January 19, 2016, mequilibrium .com/resources/new-study-reveals-the-connection-between-resilience -and-positive-business-outcomes.
3   "Why Building Resilience in Your Workplace Is Good for Business," Byte- start, bytestart.co.uk/resilient-workforce-business.html.
4   "New Study Reveals the Connection," meQuilibrium.
5   Ed Catmull, with Amy Wallace, *Creativity, Inc: Overcoming the Unseen Forces That Stand in the Way of True Inspiration* (London: Bantam Press, 2014).
6   Ed Catmull, "Inside the Pixar Braintrust," *Fast Company*, March 12, 2014, fastcompany.com/3027135/inside-the-pixar-braintrust.
7   Catmull, "Inside the Pixar Braintrust."
8   Catmull, *Creativity, Inc.*
9   "Pixar Employee Reviews," Indeed, indeed.com/cmp/Pixar/reviews.
10   Sheila Heen and Douglas Stone, "Find the Coaching in Criticism," *Harvard Business Review* (January–February 2014), hbr.org/2014/01/find -the-coaching-in-criticism.
11   Tom Nolan, "The No. 1 Employee Benefit That No One's Talking About," Gallup, Workplace, gallup.com/workplace/232955/no-employee-benefit -no-one-talking.aspx.

5: Claiming Values

1   Viola Davis quoted in Kristina Rodulfo, "21 of Viola Davis's Most Inspiring Quotes," *Elle*, January 6, 2017, elle.com/culture/celebrities/a33069/viola-davis-inspiring-quotes.

2   "Alignment and Engagement: It's All About Heads and Hearts," Imaginasium, imaginasium.com/blog/alignment-and-engagement-its-all-about-heads-and-hearts.

3   As cited in "The Impact of Employee Engagement on Productivity," Engagedly, engagedly.com/impact-of-employee-engagement-on-productivity.

4   Simon Sinek, *Start with Why: How Great Leaders Inspire Everyone to Take Action* (New York: Portfolio, 2009).

5   Interview with Jane Finette, co-founder, be radical, conducted by Barlow Initiatives, November 2019.

6   James Archer, "20 Words You Can Drop from Your Core Values Right Now," *Inc.*, January 22, 2014, inc.com/james-archer/20-words-you-can-drop-from-your-core-values-right-now.html.

7   Tyler Bosmeny, "Clever Is a Group Project and an *Inc.* 2019 Best Workplace," Clever, blog, May 2019, blog.clever.com/2019/05/clever-is-a-group-project-and-an-inc-2019-best-workplace.

8   Stephen R. Covey, *The 7 Habits of Highly Effective People: Powerful Lessons in Personal Change*, 25th anniversary ed. (New York: Simon & Schuster, 2004), 132.

9   Interview with Mary Colvig, head of ops, James Beauty, conducted by Barlow Initiatives, November 2019.

10 Leland Franklin, email message to Debbie Cohen, August 15, 2020.

6: Owning Your Impact

1   "Lululemon Founder Chip Wilson Issues Apology following Thigh-Rubbing Pants Comments," CBC News, November 13, 2013, cbsnews.com/news/lululemon-founder-chip-wilson-issues-apology-following-thigh-rubbing-pants-comments/.

2   Heidi Grant Halvorson, *No One Understands You and What to Do About It* (Boston: Harvard Business Review Press, 2015), 2, 4.

3   David Baker, "Accountability: Five Ways CEOs Fail Their Employees," Think Shift, August 15, 2017, thinkshiftinc.com/blog/top-accountability-fails-made-by-ceos.

4   Darren Overfield and Rob Kaiser, "One Out of Every Two Managers Is Terrible at Accountability," *Harvard Business Review*, November 8, 2012, hbr.org/2012/11/one-out-of-every-two-managers-is-terrible-at-accountability.

5 Sean Pomeroy, "Why Accountability Matters in the Workplace," Talent-Culture, October 6, 2015, talentculture.com/why-accountability-in-the-workplace-matters.

6 Interview with Pascal Finette, co-founder, be radical, conducted by Barlow Initiatives, November 2019.

7 Michael O'Malley, "What the 'Best Companies to Work For' Do Differently," *Harvard Business Review*, December 12, 2019, hbr.org/2019/12/what-the-best-companies-to-work-for-do-differently.

8 O'Malley, "What the 'Best Companies to Work For' Do Differently."

9 Interview with Billy Kilmer, founder, Charge EPC, conducted by Barlow Initiatives, February 2021.

10 Susan Cain, *Quiet: The Power of Introverts in a World That Can't Stop Talking* (New York: Crown, 2012), 51.

11 "Leader Isolation: 6 Ways to Conquer Loneliness at the Top," RapidStart Leadership, 2020, rapidstartleadership.com/leader-isolation.

7: Daring Not to Know

1 Adapted from an exercise by Tom Courry, owner, The Next Level (CTI leadership training, Sebastopol, CA, 2004).

2 Elizabeth Anderson, "10 Ignored Warnings That Were Tragically Deadly," Listverse, May 12, 2016, listverse.com/2016/05/12/10-ignored-warnings-that-turned-deadly.

3 Michael D. Watkins and Max H. Bazerman, "Predictable Surprises: The Disasters You Should Have Seen Coming," *Harvard Business Review*, April 2003, hbr.org/2003/04/predictable-surprises-the-disasters-you-should-have-seen-coming.

4 Gill Corkindale, "Overcoming Imposter Syndrome," *Harvard Business Review*, May 7, 2008, hbr.org/2008/05/overcoming-imposter-syndrome.

5 Kevin Cashman, *Leadership from the Inside Out: Becoming a Leader for Life*, 2nd ed. (San Francisco: Berrett-Koehler, 2008), 52.

6 "Alignment and Engagement," Imaginasium.

7 As cited in "The Impact of Employee Engagement on Productivity," Engagedly.

8 Tony Boatman, "How Employee Engagement and Productivity Are Related," ConnectSolutions, July 27, 2017, connectsolutions.ch/blog/how-employee-engagement-and-productivity-are-related.

9 Susan Sorenson, "How Employee Engagement Drives Growth," Gallup, Workplace, June 20, 2013, gallup.com/workplace/236927/employee-engagement-drives-growth.aspx.

10 Bill Howatt, "What's the Cost of Having Unproductive Employees?" *Globe and Mail*, February 6, 2015, theglobeandmail.com/report-on-business/careers/career-advice/life-at-work/productivity-table/article22192638.

11 Elizabeth Dukes, "Employee Engagement and Employee Productivity Aren't the Same Thing—Here's How to Boost Both," *Forbes*, January 12, 2018, forbes.com/sites/forbestechcouncil/2018/01/12/employee-engagement -and-employee-productivity-arent-the-same-thing-heres-how-to-boost -both/#35f29a73891b.

12 Peter Cappelli and Liat Eldor, "Where Measuring Engagement Goes Wrong," *Harvard Business Review*, May 17, 2019, hbr.org/2019/05/where -measuring-engagement-goes-wrong.

13 Michael Bungay Stanier, *The Coaching Habit: Say Less, Ask More & Change the Way You Lead Forever* (Vancouver: Page Two, 2016), 58–59.

14 Interview with Joan Burke, CPO, DocuSign, conducted by Barlow Initiatives, November 2019.

15 Eli Watkins, "Bush and Clinton Stress Value of Humility in Oval Office," CNN, Politics, July 14, 2017, cnn.com/2017/07/13/politics/george-w-bush -bill-clinton-dallas.

16 Chris Nichols, Shoma Chatterjee Hayden and Chris Trendler, "4 Behaviors That Help Leaders Manage a Crisis," *Harvard Business Review*, April 2, 2020, hbr.org/2020/04/4-behaviors-that-help-leaders-manage-a-crisis.

17 "How Leaders Can Maximize Trust and Minimize Stress during the COVID-19 Pandemic," American Psychological Association, March 20, 2020, apa.org/news/apa/2020/03/covid-19-leadership.

18 Daniel Goleman, *Emotional Intelligence: Why It Can Matter More Than IQ*, 10th anniversary ed. (New York: Bantam, 2005).

19 Brené Brown, *Daring Greatly: How the Courage to Be Vulnerable Transforms the Way We Live, Love, Parent, and Lead* (New York: Gotham Books, 2012).

20 Adapted from an exercise by Tom Courry, The Next Level.

index

about the authors

Debbie Cohen

Debbie's beliefs about human potential are grounded in decades of work with humans big and small. Her career began as a teacher and leader of early childhood education programs at Stanford University and the USGS. This era shaped her thinking about how humans grow and evolve, and the role environments play. She moved on, applying these ideas to building strategies with companies seeking to attract and retain key talent through work/life initiatives. This work heightened her awareness of systemic roadblocks and the impact they have on people and productivity. Shifting from consulting to internal work, Debbie began leading work/life for Time Warner just after the infamous AOL/Time Warner merger. She became known for getting groups who did not typically work well together to a place of shared focus and effort. This ignited a bigger shift into executive leadership roles in HR at Time Warner, Razorfish, Mozilla and First Look LLC. The impact of Debbie's work was recognized in a case study released by Harvard Business Publishing, *People Operations at Mozilla*

Corporation: Scaling a Peer-to-Peer Global Community, which received the 2014 Berkeley Haas Best Case Award for the most important contribution to management education.

Kate Roeske-Zummer

Kate knows vulnerability-based leadership creates stronger relationships, more authentic connections and better results. As an account manager at Ogilvy & Mather, Kate recognized the power in distributing responsibility to the people on her team. She experienced first-hand that the whole of a team really is greater than the sum of its parts. Eventually, Kate experienced the fatigue that comes from working in a system where conversations repeat and go nowhere. So, she changed what she could—where she put her focus. She let go of her advertising career and in 2003 she became a certified coach back when folks only associated the term "coach" with sports! Several decades and hundreds of clients later, Kate remains steadfast in her calling to support people on their journey to becoming the humans they want to be. She knows the power of coaching to help people overcome their internal roadblocks; this is her purpose in life. Kate is now a master coach, even devoting eight years to training other coaches on the faculty of Co-Active Training Institute (CTI). She has brought her skills to organizations including Mozilla, Pinterest, Adobe, DaVita, CBS Interactive, United Way of America, Intuit, Clever, Charge EPC and Articulate. She has a master's degree from the University of Cambridge, England.

HumanityWorks

HUMANITYWORKS helps organizations improve workplace productivity. Working together is messy and most people don't know how to navigate this well, which results in behaviors that create toxicity and roadblocks that stall productivity. Yet when working together is deeper and more connected, people give more of themselves and business wins. We provide straightforward, practical techniques that shift behavior to be a good human and do better work, allowing you and your organization to thrive.

Find out more at **humanityworks.com**.

Join the Movement

Join our email list and become part of the community of people looking to be good humans, do better work and help create places where humanity works better. Details and additional resources are found on our website (humanityworks.com).

Self-directed action

Throughout the book, there are exercises you can practice and tools you can use to begin to shift your behavior to bring more humanity to the workplace and into your life.

- *Humanity Works Better* **workbook:** For those who want a deeper exploration into the concepts, skills and tools in *Humanity Works Better* and are interested in a self-paced journey, this workbook is for you! We deconstruct the four mindset shifts and Five Practices, and provide additional practical techniques to shift behavior so that you can be a model of how humanity works better.

- **Podcasts and articles:** Looking for a little pick-me-up and inspiration to keep you going on your journey? Subscribe to our podcasts or receive regular articles from Humanity-Works. Our archive is available on our website.

Group action

When you are looking to lead your teams with bigger impact, we offer several tools to support your journey. All of these resources are available on our website.

- **Book group guide:** For those who have a few friends or colleagues along for the journey, the *Humanity Works Better* book group guide offers powerful questions to deepen personal insights and awareness, make choices and champion one another with the courage to change.

- **Small teams workbooks:** If you lead a team or a series of teams and want to arm them with skills and techniques to bring more humanity into your workplace, HumanityWorks offers a facilitator guide and workbooks designed for leaders and their teams to make the journey together.

Culture shifts

If you want to lead the humanity works better charge at your organization, please contact us to learn more about our offerings:

- **Humanity Works Better Program:** To create a healthy and humane workplace culture, we offer a series of programs tailored to the needs of different audiences, from the C-suite to individual contributors. Our team of consultants is trained to deliver the Humanity Works Better Program for your teams, leaders and organization.

- **Claim your spot:** Become certified as an organization/company where humanity works better. This recognition is ideal for recruiting and retaining other great humans dedicated to bringing more humanity to the workplace.